D0259921

Excel
Made Easy

A beginner's guide including how-to skills and projects

Ewan Arthur

Withdrawn Stock
Dorset Libraries

ARCTURUS

DORSET COUNTY LIBRARY

400 197 422 T

Contents

Introduction   3 – 9

1 First steps

Launching **Excel** – Opening workbooks   10 – 11
Using the Cloud – Project   12 – 13
A head start   14 – 15
Moving around – Project   16 – 17

2 Foundations

First words – Series fun   18 – 19
Fonts and points – Project   20 – 21
Styles – Which way in cells   22 – 23
Set your table – Project   24 – 25
A bigger table – A smaller table   26 – 27
Sorting and reordering – Project   28 – 29
Use a flash filling   30 – 31

3 Presentation

Make your table stand out – Make cells stand out   32 – 33
Styling cells – Project   34 – 35
Styling tables – Table style options   36 – 37

4 Get it out there

How it looks on paper – Print part of your work   38 – 39
Long or wide – Project   40 – 41
Tools for better printing – Print your document   42 – 43

5 Speed it up

Copy and paste – Moving   44 – 45
Turn back time – Project   46 – 47
The history of copying   48 – 49
Copy just the value – Project   50 – 51
Copy just the style – Linking together   52 – 53
Check your text – Project   54 – 55

6 Maths and methods

Simple sums – Start the power   56 – 57
Start the power – Project   58 – 59

Build up steam   60 – 61
Total Power – Project   62 – 63
Formulas and functions – Number and number   64 – 65
Number and number – Project   66 – 67
Setting a date   68 – 69

7 Charts and graphs

Visualize your data – Design your chart   70 – 71
What are you looking at? – Project   72 – 73
More layout options   74 – 75
More Format options – Project   76 – 77
Mmmm, pie (charts)!   78 – 79
Let **Excel** decide – Project   80 – 81
Speed through charts   82 – 83

8 Data tricks

Using fast mini-graphs   84 – 85
Show it quickly – Project   86 – 87
Rich data labels   88 – 89
A slice of table – Project   90 – 91
Pivot your chart   92 – 93

9 Final touches

Adding graphics   94 – 95
Picture your PC – Project   96 – 97
Text effects   98 – 99
Print headers – Project   100 – 101
Quick chart change – Future bookings   102 – 103

10 Work online

Sharing online   104 – 105
No Excel? – Project   106 – 107
Can anybody help me?   108 – 109

11 Good to know

Help is always there   110 – 111

Index   112

2

How to use this book

This book will help you learn how to use Microsoft **Excel**, probably the most popular spreadsheet software in the world.

- It is written for beginners and covers only what you really need.

- There's no jargon, just simple instructions and lots of pictures.
  You'll start with the basics and soon be able to make tables and charts, do maths and manage money.

Step-by-step skills pages

These pages explain each skill and the steps needed to use the skill.

Pictures show you what's on your computer screen.*

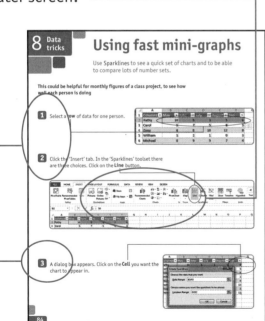

Project pages

These pages get you to practise the skills in a series of fun projects.

The projects are explained with step-by-step instructions and pictures.

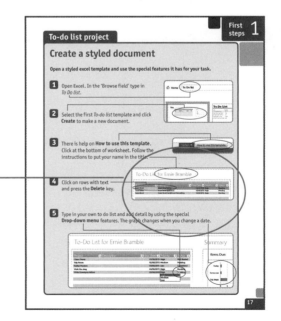

---

* *Some images are combined to show what the outcome of the action shown will be.*

The Microsoft Office Excel window

What you will see when you open an **Excel** document:

The File tab. Click this to do things to the whole document such as save it. You can also customise how **Excel** works.

The Ribbon – where most of the options that you will learn about are found.

The Quick Access toolbar – does most common tasks such as Open and Save, but without any options.

The Formula Bar – shows you the calculation (formula), number or text inside a cell.

The Close button. Click to exit **Excel**.

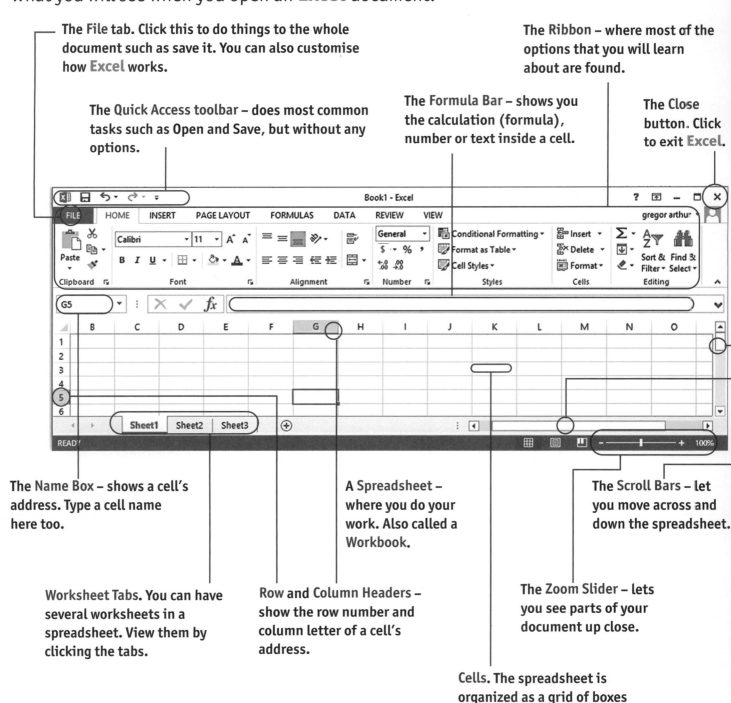

The Name Box – shows a cell's address. Type a cell name here too.

A Spreadsheet – where you do your work. Also called a Workbook.

The Scroll Bars – let you move across and down the spreadsheet.

Worksheet Tabs. You can have several worksheets in a spreadsheet. View them by clicking the tabs.

Row and Column Headers – show the row number and column letter of a cell's address.

The Zoom Slider – lets you see parts of your document up close.

Cells. The spreadsheet is organized as a grid of boxes called cells.

The Ribbon

The **Ribbon** is where to find most of the tools you use. The ribbon is divided into **tabs**. Each tab is split up into sets of **tools**. **Excel** is clever and depending on what you are doing, puts useful tabs in the ribbon.

The File tab. This opens the 'Backstage' area, where you create and save your documents.

A Button.

A Button Drop-down Menu – shows options related to a button.

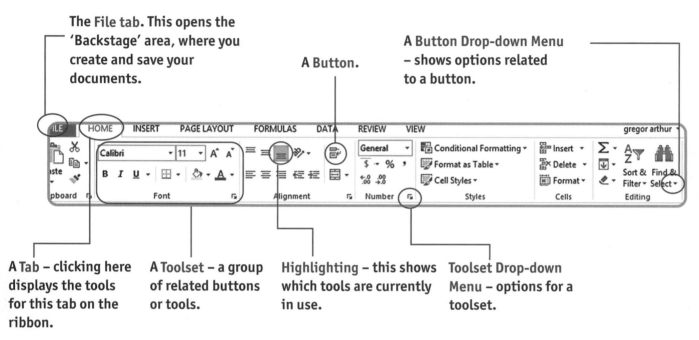

A Tab – clicking here displays the tools for this tab on the ribbon.

A Toolset – a group of related buttons or tools.

Highlighting – this shows which tools are currently in use.

Toolset Drop-down Menu – options for a toolset.

Starting Excel

What to do to get **Excel** running on your computer.

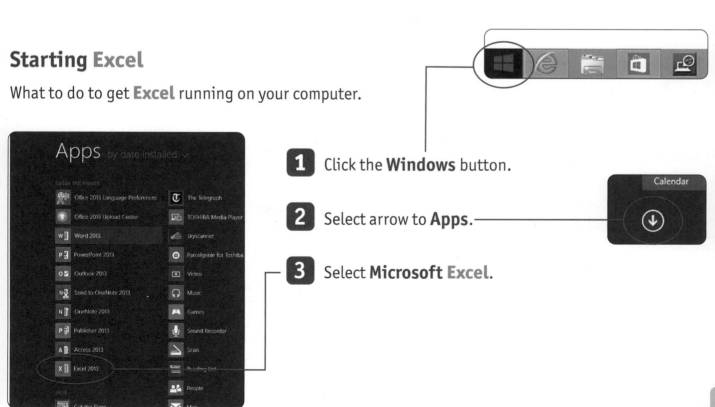

1 Click the **Windows** button.

2 Select arrow to **Apps**.

3 Select **Microsoft Excel**.

Using the mouse

You will use a mouse and keyboard with **Excel**. You can often use either to do the same thing. For example, get help by pressing the **F1** function key or clicking on the **?** icon.

Common terms and techniques

Right-click – press and release the <u>right</u>-hand button.

Click – press and release the <u>left</u>-hand button. Two quick clicks is a Double-Click.

Click-and-drag – press the left mouse button, move (or drag) the cursor, then release it. This either highlights everything covered or moves whatever was selected by the first click.

Mouse pointer – moving the mouse moves the mouse pointer around the screen. It changes depending on what is going on.

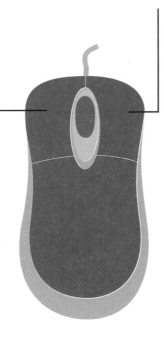

Cursor – The flashing line (cursor) shows where type will appear when entered.

Hover-over – keep the mouse pointer over a button for a few seconds. This will often produce a pop-up message.

Using the keyboard

Common terms and techniques

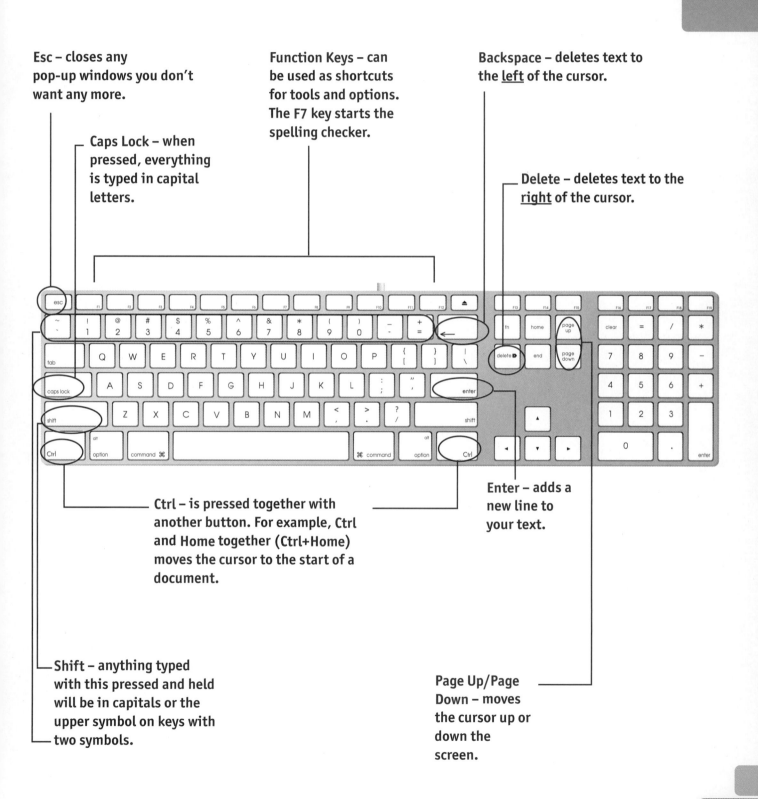

Esc – closes any pop-up windows you don't want any more.

Caps Lock – when pressed, everything is typed in capital letters.

Function Keys – can be used as shortcuts for tools and options. The F7 key starts the spelling checker.

Backspace – deletes text to the <u>left</u> of the cursor.

Delete – deletes text to the <u>right</u> of the cursor.

Ctrl – is pressed together with another button. For example, Ctrl and Home together (Ctrl+Home) moves the cursor to the start of a document.

Enter – adds a new line to your text.

Shift – anything typed with this pressed and held will be in capitals or the upper symbol on keys with two symbols.

Page Up/Page Down – moves the cursor up or down the screen.

Excel on touch screens

Excel can work on a touch screen as well as a PC computer. You can change between *Mouse Mode* and *Touch Mode*. This will help make it easier to use touch-screen commands.

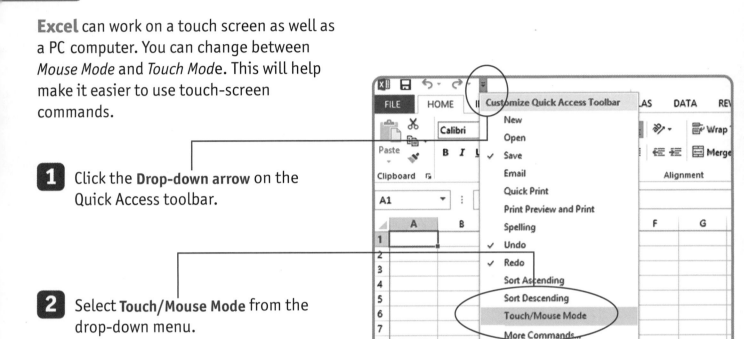

1 Click the **Drop-down arrow** on the Quick Access toolbar.

2 Select **Touch/Mouse Mode** from the drop-down menu.

3 Select **Touch** from the drop-down menu.

4 The Ribbon switches to **Touch Mode**. You will see more space around the buttons.

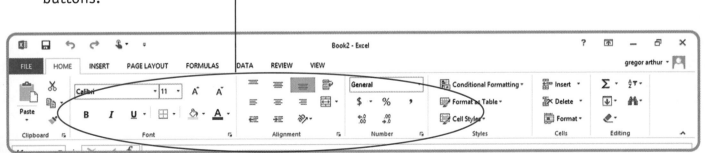

Common terms and techniques

There are different versions of **Excel** for tablets. Here are three ways of using your fingers to interact with a touch-screen device:

Tapping

One tap on an item opens, or activates it the same way a mouse click does.

Stretching

Touching the screen with two fingers and stretching them apart will zoom in, making things bigger.

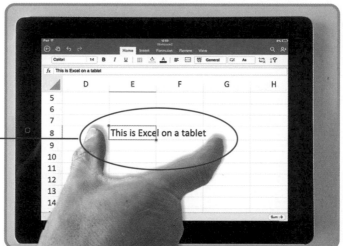

Copying and Pasting

Press on a cell and hold to see options. You can copy cells this way to paste somewhere else.

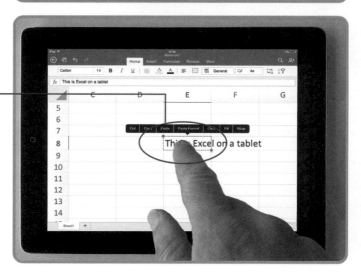

Launching Excel

Creating and Saving workbooks

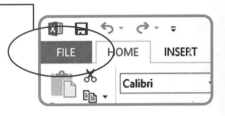

1 Click on the **File** tab.

2 Click on **New** to view the new Workbook options.

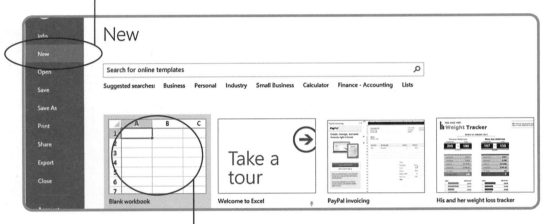

3 Double-click on **Blank workbook**.

4 Click on a cell in the new spreadsheet, type something and press the **Enter** key.

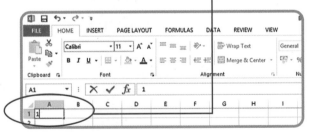

5 To save the workbook, click **Save As** in the **File** tab.

6 A dialog box opens. A default name 'Book1' is given to your file, but you can give it a name to help identify it. Then click **Save**.

Opening workbooks

Open a workbook and Save As a
different workbook

Your existing files may need to be copied.

1 Click the **File** tab and then on the **Open** button.

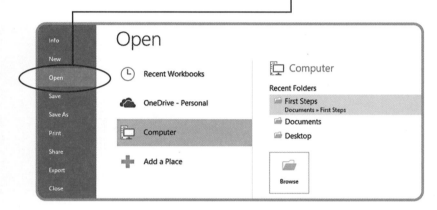

Top Tip!

The **File** tab opens showing
recent documents.
Double-click on these to
open them.

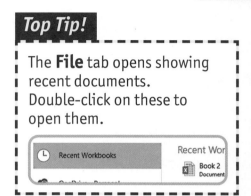

2 A dialog box opens showing the
Excel files in your *Documents* folder.
Click on the workbook you want to
use, then on the **Open** button.

3 Click on the **File** tab and then **Save As**.

4 In the 'Save As' dialog box, click the **New folder**
button to create a folder to save your files in.
Name it *My spreadsheets*. Select the
File name.

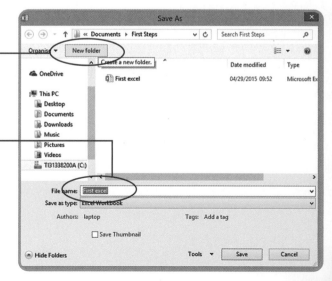

5 Change the 'File name' to *Second Excel*.

Using the Cloud

Save your spreadsheet to the Internet and open it again

If you save your work to the Cloud you can open it from any computer with access to the Internet and share it with other people.

1 Open a document and click on the **File** tab. Select **Save As** and then your Cloud **OneDrive** location.

2 Click **Browse** to create a new online folder.

3 A dialog box appears of your **OneDrive folder** window. Create a **New folder** inside it.

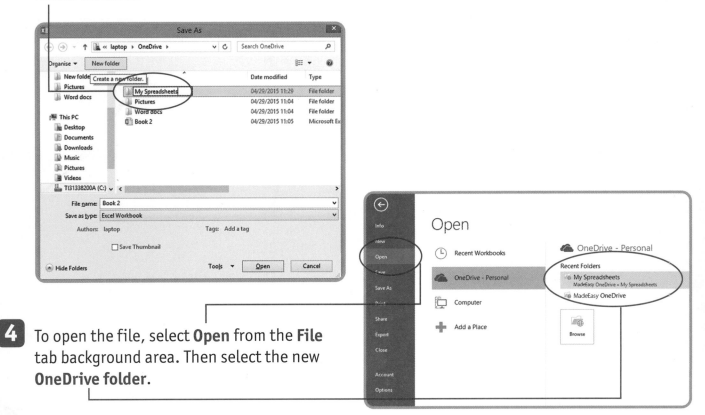

4 To open the file, select **Open** from the **File** tab background area. Then select the new **OneDrive folder**.

To-do list project

A simple first spreadsheet

Start a spreadsheet, add information and save it.
Use the Cloud to store your to-dos and open them again.

1 Open a new spreadsheet. Enter your first to-do in cell **B4**.

2 Press the **Enter** key. This will move you to the cell below; **B5**.

3 Add your other jobs to your list.

4 Click on cell **A4** and enter the day when you have to do each thing on the list.

5 Save your work as *My To-do list 1*.

6 Close the spreadsheet and **Excel** using the **Close** button.

7 Open your *My To-do list 1* spreadsheet. Save your workbook to your *My Spreadsheets* folder in your **OneDrive**.

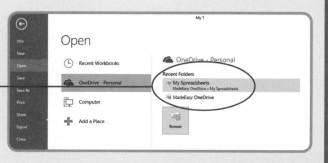

A head start

You can use templates to create a
styled document

**Excel templates are a very quick way of creating many types of document
for most of your needs.**

1 Select the 'File' tab and go to **New**
in the drop-down menu.

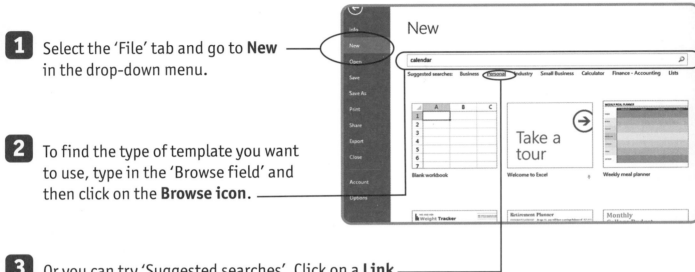

2 To find the type of template you want
to use, type in the 'Browse field' and
then click on the **Browse icon**.

3 Or you can try 'Suggested searches'. Click on a **Link**
to a category.

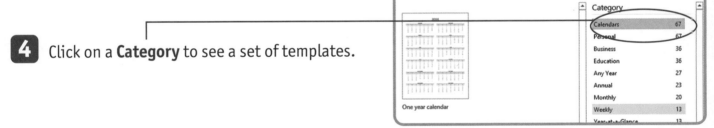

4 Click on a **Category** to see a set of templates.

5 Select the template you want.
It will appear in a 'slideshow'
window. Click **Create**
to open the template.

*You can start using the template
straight away!*

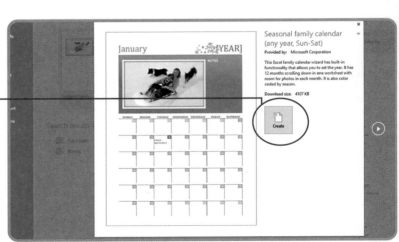

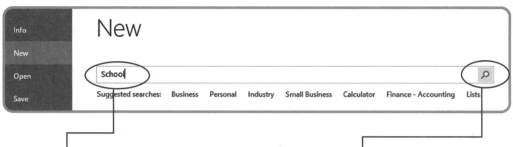

6 Type 'School' in the search field and click on the **Browse** icon. Click the 'Back to School Checklist' template and click **Create**.

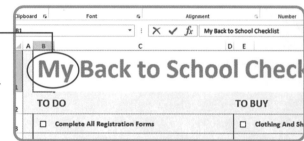

7 Double click at the start of the title 'Back to School Checklist'. The title is selected. You can change it and then press **OK**.

8 Click-and-drag on the 'To Do' column. Whatever you select will go gray. Click the **Delete** Key. The text disappears.

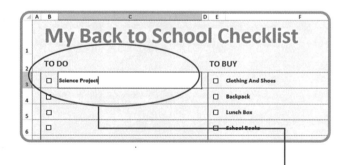

9 Click on the top 'To do'. You can now type in your own reminders. Press **OK** when each is done. The next is selected for you. Click on a tick box. **Excel** adds a tick for you.

Save your work as *My Checklist*.

TO DO		TO BUY
☑ Science Project		☐ Clothing A...
☐ Watch a film at the movie theater		☐ Backpack
☐ Try some new food like vegetables!		☐ Lunch Box
☑ Soccer practice		☑ School Boo...
☐ Guitar practice		☐ Folders
☐		☐ Pens, Penc...

Moving around

Moving around and **deleting** using the mouse and keyboard

You will make mistakes. Here's how to move around a spreadsheet to delete things.

1 Move from one cell to another by clicking in that cell or using the keyboard arrow keys.

Right arrow key 3 times

A1	▼	⋮	✕ ✓	*fx*	Start Cell

	A	B	C	D	E
1	Start Cell				
2					
3					
4					
5					
6					
7					

Down arrow key 3 times

2 Click-and-drag the 'Scroll Bar' or press the **Page Up** or **Page Down** keys to move up and down.

3 Press the **Delete** key to delete everything in a cell.

4 Delete several cells by click-and-dragging the mouse pointer across them, then pressing the **Delete** key.

To select several cells, press and hold the left mouse button down.

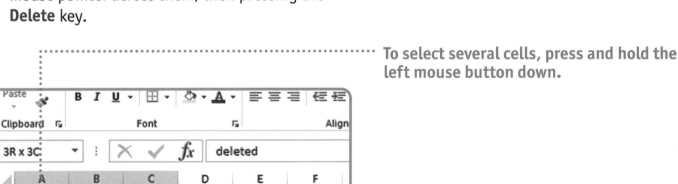

Paste		B *I* <u>U</u> ▾	⊞ ▾	◇ ▾ **A** ▾	≡ ≡ ≡	⇤ ⇥
Clipboard ⌐			Font	⌐		Align

3R x 3C	▼	⋮	✕ ✓	*fx*	deleted

	A	B	C	D	E	F
1	all	of	these			
2	cells	are	going			
3	to	be	deleted			
4						

Then move your mouse around to here and release the button.

To-do list project

Create a styled document

Open a styled Excel template and use the special features it has for your task.

1 Open **Excel**. In the 'Browse field' type in *To Do list*.

⌂ Home | To Do list

2 Select the first *To-do list* template and click **Create** to make a new document.

3 There is help on **How to use this template**. Click at the bottom of the worksheet. Follow the instructions to put your name in the title. ——

To-Do-List | How to use this template

4 Click on rows with text —— and press the **Delete** key.

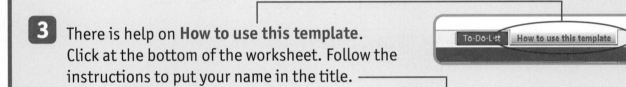

To-Do List for Ernie Bramble

Project	Description	Due Date	Priority	Status
Learn Excel	Learn Excel Tables	6/1/2016	High	Pending
Learn Excel	Learn Excel Sparklines	6/2/2016	High	Pending
Learn Excel	Learn Excel Conditional Formatting	6/3/2016	High	Pending

5 Type in your own to-do list and add detail by using the special **Drop-down menu** features. The graph changes when you change a date.

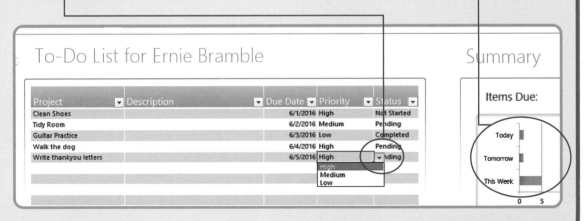

To-Do List for Ernie Bramble

Project	Description	Due Date	Priority	Status
Clean Shoes		6/1/2016	High	Not Started
Tidy Room		6/2/2016	Medium	Pending
Guitar Practice		6/3/2016	Low	Completed
Walk the dog		6/4/2016	High	Pending
Write thankyou letters		6/5/2016	High	Pending

High
Medium
Low

Summary

Items Due:

Today
Tomorrow
This Week

0   5

First words

Cells and the Formula Bar

You can edit text once it is entered in a cell.

1 Open a new spreadsheet.

2 Click on a cell and type a sentence.

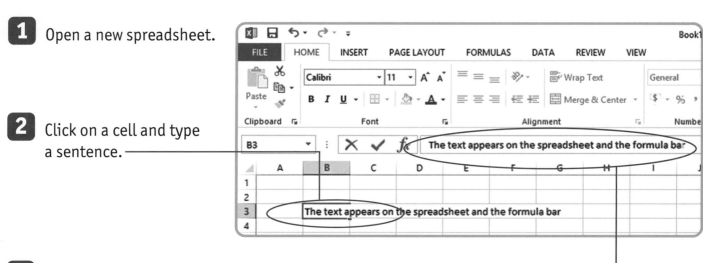

3 The text appears both in the cell and the 'Formula Bar'.

4 To edit a cell, double-click on the cell. Press the **F2** key or click on the 'Formula Bar'.

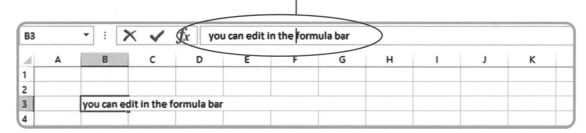

5 When editing a cell, use the **Arrow**, **Backspace** and **Delete** keys to move around.

6 Press the **Enter** key to finish.

Top Tip!

If you can't see a file name in the 'Open' dialog box, click-and-drag the bottom right corner of the box to make it bigger.

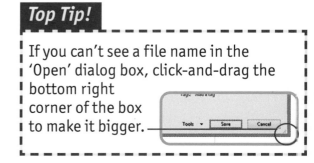

Series fun

Use Auto Fill to complete a series

Excel can complete series, such as numbers and dates, automatically.

1 Open a workbook. Type *1, 2, 3* in three cells.

2 Select these cells.

3 Hover-over the small square at the bottom right of your selection until the mouse pointer turns into the 'Auto Fill' cross.

4 Click-and-drag the 'Auto Fill' cross downwards. **Excel** automatically fills in the next numbers in the series.

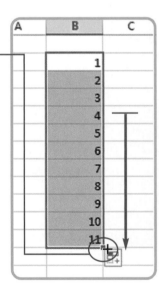

5 **Excel** can 'Auto Fill' dates too. Type *Mon, Tue, Wed* then use 'Auto Fill' to add the other five days of the week and more.

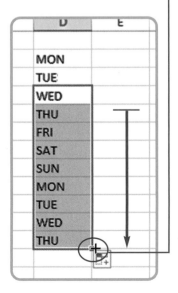

Top Tip!

To add a new worksheet, click on the **New Sheet** button at the bottom of the window. Double-click on the **Sheet** name to change it.

Fonts and points

Changing Fonts and Font Sizes

Fonts are styles of text. The size is in points. The normal size is 11 point, but you can go from 1 to 409 point.

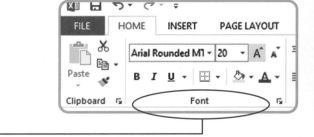

1 Go to the 'Font' toolset on the **Home** tab.

2 Click the **Font** button drop-down menu and select a new **Font**.

3 Start typing in a cell. The text will appear in that font style.

This is Agency FB

4 To change the font of cell text, select it and click the **Font** button drop-down menu to choose a new font.

5 To make a text bigger or smaller choose a new size using the **Font Size** button drop-down menu or click the **Grow Font** or **Shrink Font** buttons.

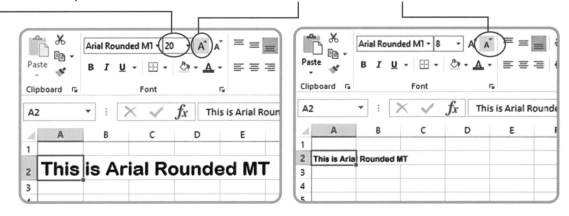

Rehearsal schedule project

Create a rehearsal schedule

Start a spreadsheet, add information and a heading style and save it.

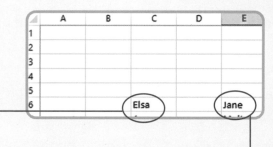

1 Start a new workbook and save as *Rehearsal Schedule 1*. Starting in cell **C6**, list the roles in your show.

2 Starting in **E6**, add the names of those who will play each role.

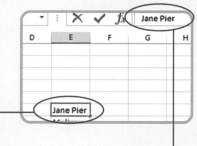

3 Edit each name to add their last name. Try using **F2**, or clicking in the **Formula Bar** or double-clicking the cell.

4 Add the rehearsal start date to cell **F5**. Add the next date in cell **G5**.

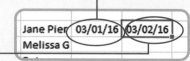

5 Select **F5** and **G5**, then 'Auto Fill' until you reach the dress rehearsal date.

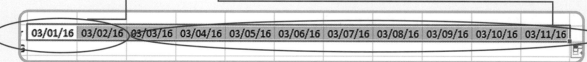

6 Type a name for your show in **C2**. Then style the title with a different font, a larger size and a new color.

Styles

Style text with Bold, Italic, Underline and Colors

'Bold', 'italic' and 'underline' make text stand out. Colors brighten things up.

1 Select a cell with text in. Click the **Bold** button on the **Home** tab. The text becomes **bold**.

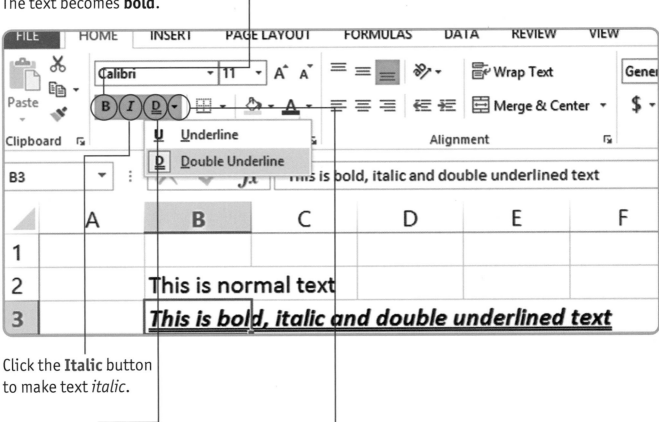

2 Click the **Italic** button to make text *italic*.

3 Click the **Underline** button to <u>underline</u> text.

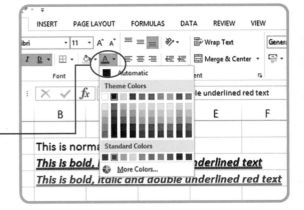

4 Choose different underline styles with the **Underline** button drop-down menu.

5 Click the **Font Color** button drop-down menu to choose a color for the text.

Which way in cells

Aligning, Merging and Wrapping text in cells

Excel starts text at the left of a cell, and numbers and dates to the right.
This is not always wanted.

1 In the **Home** tab, click the **Align Text Left** button to move numbers left in a cell.

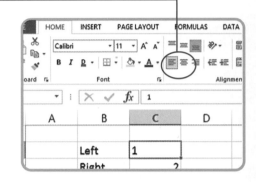

2 To move text to the center, click the **Align Text Center** button.

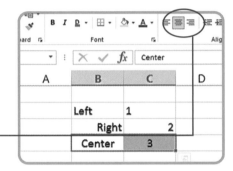

3 To type at different angles, use the **Orientation** button drop-down menu. This gives you several alignment choices.

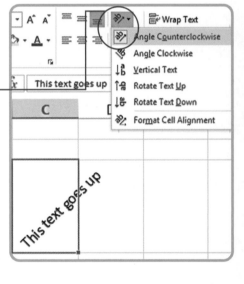

4 Use the **Wrap Text** button to get several lines into one cell.

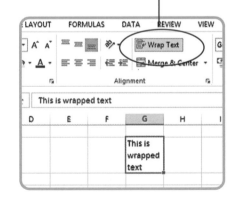

5 You can merge cells into one. Select two or more cells and click the **Merge & Center** button. They become a single large cell.

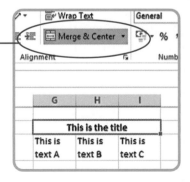

Set your table

Changing the Row Height and Column Width

Top Tip!

Double-click on the edge of a column or row header to make it automatically fit to the largest cell in that column or row.

Rows and column sizes can be changed to help work fit.

1 Place the mouse pointer between two row or column headers until it changes to a 'Double Arrow' cursor.

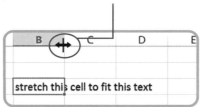

2 Click-and-drag the column or row to the size you want.

3 You can change several columns or rows at once. Select all the columns or rows by click-and-dragging over the headers.

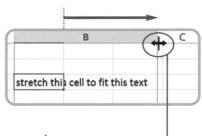

4 Then click-and-drag to resize *one* of the selected columns or rows. The others all change size too.

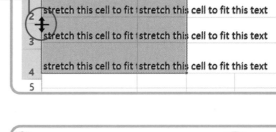

5 Click the **Format** button drop-down menu in the 'Cells' toolset, and select **Autofit Column Width**. The cells change width to fit the text.

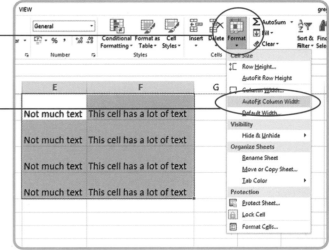

Rehearsal schedule project

Smarten the schedule

Improve your column fit and use font styles and colors.

1 Select the roles and click on the **Bold** button. Select the title and make it **Double Underlined**.

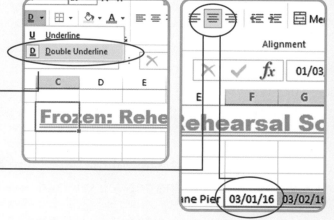

2 Select the dates and center them.

3 To center the title above your schedule, select the cells in Row 2, from column C to above your last date. Click on **Merge and Center**.

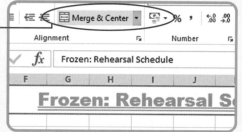

4 Use **Wrap Text** and select the names of the players.

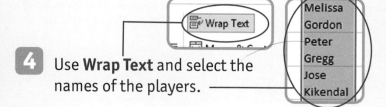

5 Increase the width of the *Role* column to fit the largest role.

6 Use the **Cell Format** tool to make the *Names* rows the same height (30 pixels).

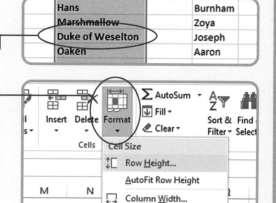

A bigger table

Inserting Rows, Columns and Cells

Sometimes you will add new columns and rows into a spreadsheet. Sometimes you will need to add just one cell.

1 To add a row or column, right-click on a row or column header and select **Insert** from the pop-up menu.

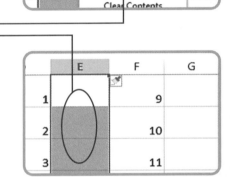

2 A new column appears to the left of the one you selected. A new row appears above the one you selected.

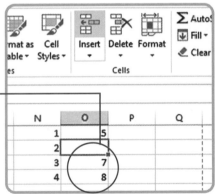

3 To add cells, select the place where you want a new cell added. Click the **Insert** button to insert a new cell. Existing cells move down below it.

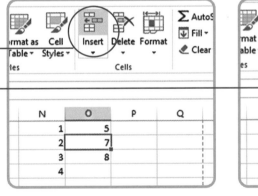

4 Select **Insert Cells** to see the 'Insert' dialog box. Select the **Shift cells right** option and click **OK** to move cells to the right of the new cell.

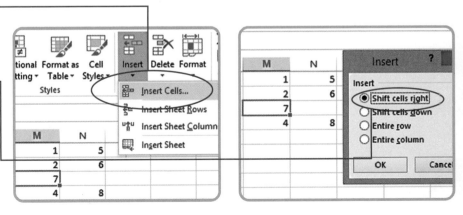

A smaller table

Deleting Rows, Columns and Cells

Sometimes you need to remove rows, columns or cells from a spreadsheet.

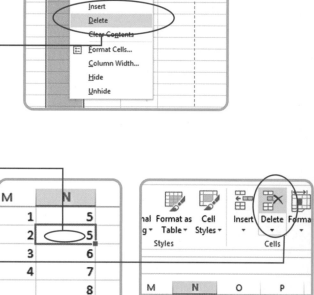

1 Right-click on the row or column header. Select **Delete**.

2 The entire row or column is deleted.

3 Delete cells by using the **Delete** button on the **Home** tab.

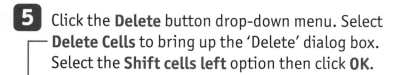

4 This moves cells below the deleted cell up.

5 Click the **Delete** button drop-down menu. Select **Delete Cells** to bring up the 'Delete' dialog box. Select the **Shift cells left** option then click **OK**.

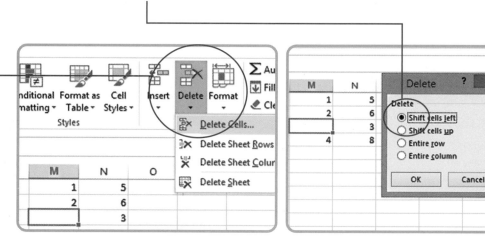
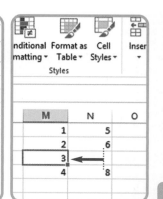

Sorting and reordering

Sorting lists into order

'Sorting' is a basic tool that makes spreadsheets useful. You can sort words, numbers and dates.

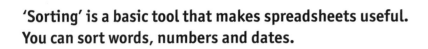

1 Type a list of fruits into a worksheet and select it. Click the **Sort & Filter** button drop-down menu from the 'Editing' toolset on the **Home** tab.

2 Select **Sort A to Z** to put them into alphabetical order. In the next column type the number of each fruit. Select the whole list.

3 Select **Custom Sort** from the **Sort & Filter** drop-down menu to sort by quantity (column **Q**). The 'Sort' dialog box appears.

4 Select the quantity column from the **Sort by** drop-down menu. Then select 'Largest to Smallest' from the **Order** drop-down menu and click **OK**. The list order changes.

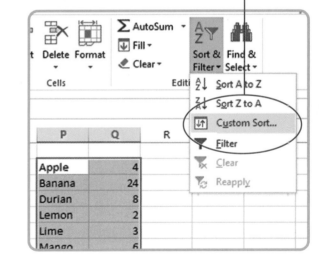

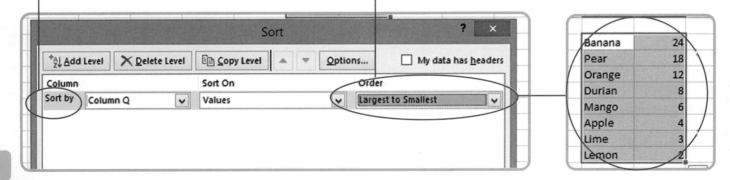

Rehearsal schedule project

Sort out rows, columns and ordering

What else can we do to the rehearsal schedule to improve it?

1 Select the first five date columns and right-click a column header to view the pop-up menu. Select **Insert.**

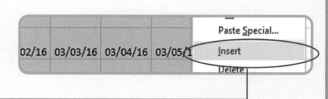

2 Add the scene names to each column. Align the scene text vertically and shrink the columns to fit.

3 Select the first role and name. Click on **Insert Cells** and select **Shift cells down.** Add titles to each column.

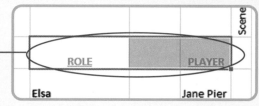

4 Select these dates and use the **Delete** tool to remove the cells. Select **Shift cells left** in the 'Delete' dialog box.

5 Select the 'Role' and 'Player' columns, including the titles, and use **Custom Sort** to sort by player name.

6 Make sure that the 'My data has headers' option is ticked. Note that you can now sort by 'Player' and not by Column C.

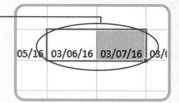

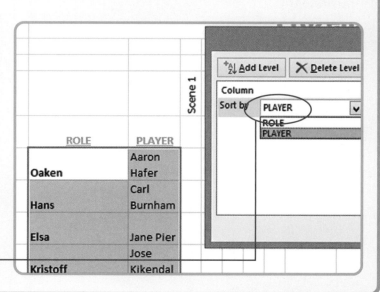

Use a flash filling

Flash Fill can tell what you want to do and do it for you.

Excel can separate or join names for you, or sort out numbers to appear similar.

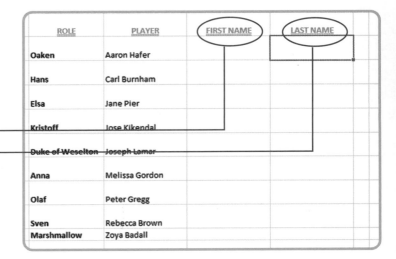

1 Open the *Rehearsal Schedule* and add two columns for *First Name* and *Last Name*.

2 Type in the top 'First name'. In the **Data** tab click **Flash Fill**. All the First Names from the *Player* column are now filled in.

3 Type in the top 'Last name'. You can also use the **Fill** drop-down menu in the 'editing' toolset of the **Home** tab. Select the **Flash Fill** option. All last names appear.

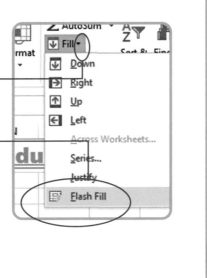

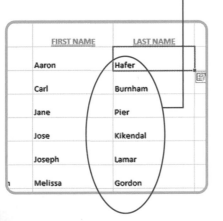

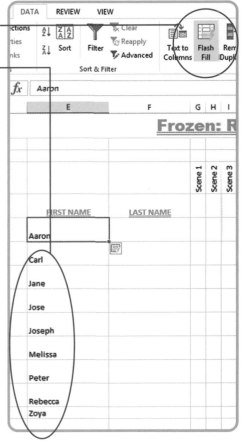

4 Add two more columns titled *Telephone*. Enter the numbers in the left-hand column. If the number starts with a zero set the 'number format' to **Text**.

5 Type the top number again but with a hyphen to format the code the right way. Select **Flash Fill**.

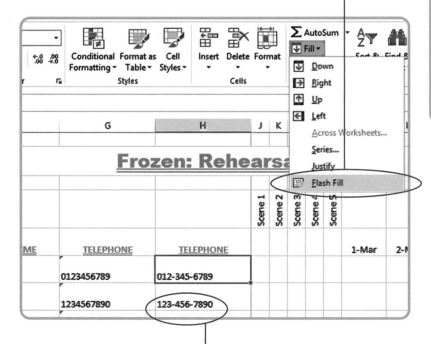

LAST NAME	TELEPHONE
Hafer	0123456789
Burnham	1234567890

...ME	TELEPHONE	TELEPHONE
	0123456789	012-345-6789
	1234567890	123-456-7890

6 **Excel** will automatically complete the second column and insert hyphens into the telephone numbers.

7 You can combine names. Type in the first name and then the player's role, in brackets, in a new column. **Flash Fill** does the rest for you.

ROLE	PLAYER	FIRST NAME	FIRST NAME (ROLE)	
Oaken	Aaron Hafer	Aaron	Aaron (Oaken)	Ha
Hans	Carl Burnham	Carl	Carl (Hans)	Bu
Elsa	Jane Pier	Jane	Jane (Elsa)	Pi
Kristoff	Jose Kikendal	Jose	Jose (Kristoff)	Ki
Duke of Weselton	Joseph Lamar	Joseph	Joseph (Duke of Weselton)	La
Anna	Melissa Gordon	Melissa	Melissa (Anna)	Go
Olaf	Peter Gregg	Peter	Peter (Olaf)	Gr
Sven	Rebecca Brown	Rebecca	Rebecca (Sven)	B
Marshmallow	Zoya Badall	Zoya	Zoya (Marshmallow)	Ba

3 Presentation

Make your table stand out

Add Borders to tables

You can make columns and rows stand out by using borders.

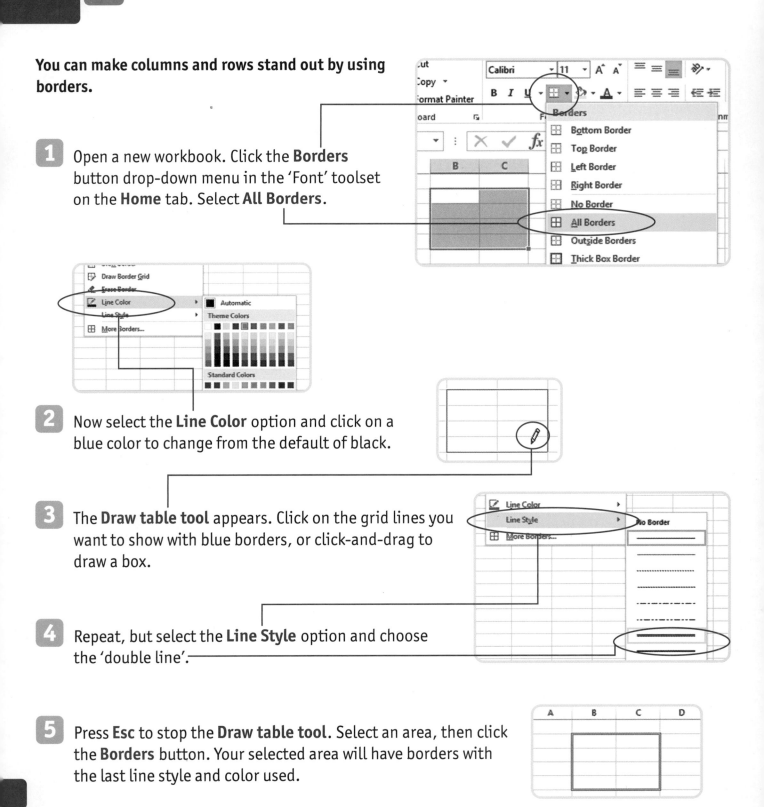

1 Open a new workbook. Click the **Borders** button drop-down menu in the 'Font' toolset on the **Home** tab. Select **All Borders**.

2 Now select the **Line Color** option and click on a blue color to change from the default of black.

3 The **Draw table tool** appears. Click on the grid lines you want to show with blue borders, or click-and-drag to draw a box.

4 Repeat, but select the **Line Style** option and choose the 'double line'.

5 Press **Esc** to stop the **Draw table tool**. Select an area, then click the **Borders** button. Your selected area will have borders with the last line style and color used.

Make cells stand out

Fill cells with background color

Color cell backgrounds to make them stand out.

1 Click on a range of cells in a spreadsheet.

2 Click the **Fill Color** button on the **Home** tab.

3 The cells' background color becomes default yellow.

4 Click the **Fill Color** button drop-down menu to get more colors.

5 Select a new color. It will be used next time you click the **Fill Color** button.

6 Select **More Colors** to see the 'Colors' dialog box and select a shade different to the 'Theme Colors' or 'Standard Colors'.

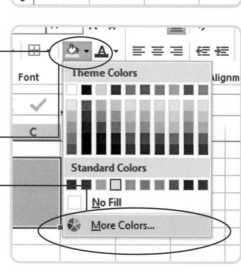

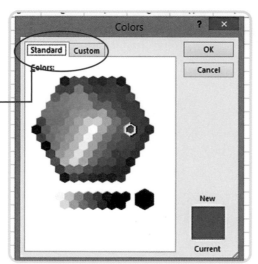

Styling cells

Use **Styles** to change the format of a cell

Styles are easy-to-apply, preset combinations of fonts and alignments.

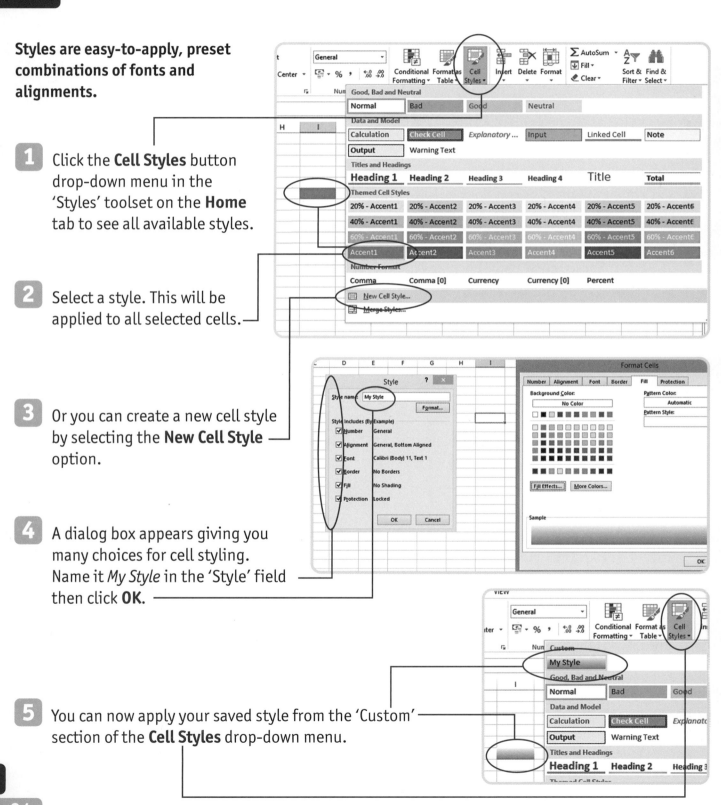

1 Click the **Cell Styles** button drop-down menu in the 'Styles' toolset on the **Home** tab to see all available styles.

2 Select a style. This will be applied to all selected cells.

3 Or you can create a new cell style by selecting the **New Cell Style** option.

4 A dialog box appears giving you many choices for cell styling. Name it *My Style* in the 'Style' field then click **OK**.

5 You can now apply your saved style from the 'Custom' section of the **Cell Styles** drop-down menu.

Revision plan project

Get your revision organized

Create your plan with splashes of color; using styles you can color it very quickly.

1 Make a new workbook, *Revision Timetable*, with subjects and dates as shown.

2 Select all and use the **Borders** drop-down menu to set 'All Borders' to thin black lines.

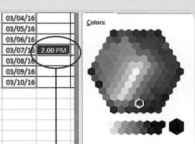

3 Change the line color to blue and with a thick outline. Select the subjects and click the **Borders** button. Repeat for the dates.

4 Insert a test time and click on the 'Fill Color' button drop-down menu to make the cell red. Style the text *white bold*.

5 Give your plan a title. **Merge & Center** it across the plan and use **Cell Style** *Heading 1*.

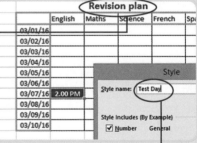

6 Select the red cell and click on **New Cell Style** in the **Cell Style** drop-down menu. Call the new style *Test Day*.

7 Press the **OK** key and then select the other tests. Apply your custom style.

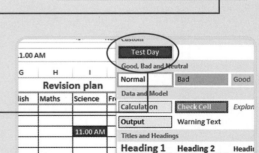

Styling tables

Use **Table Styles** for quick, good-looking tables

**'Table Styles' are a quick way to create good-looking tables.
They also add useful sort and calculation functions.**

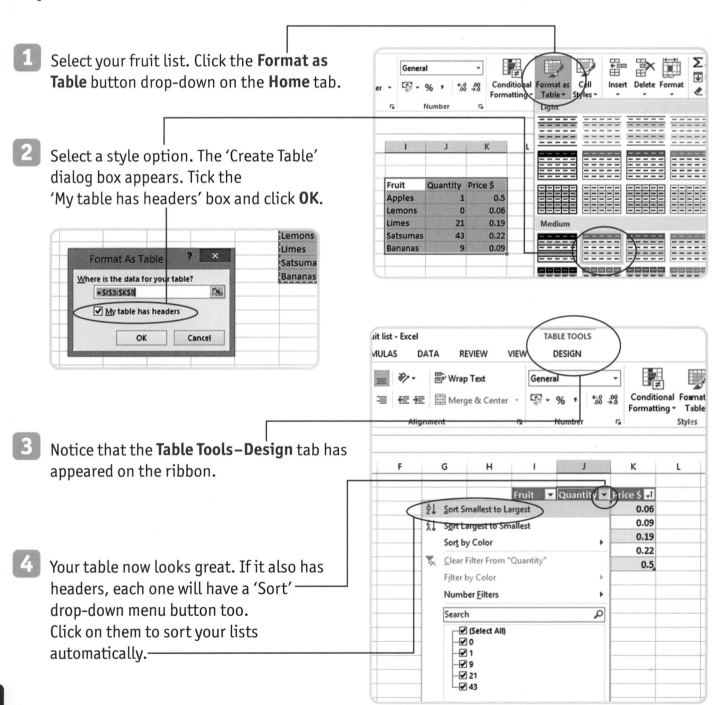

1 Select your fruit list. Click the **Format as Table** button drop-down on the **Home** tab.

2 Select a style option. The 'Create Table' dialog box appears. Tick the 'My table has headers' box and click **OK**.

3 Notice that the **Table Tools–Design** tab has appeared on the ribbon.

4 Your table now looks great. If it also has headers, each one will have a 'Sort' drop-down menu button too. Click on them to sort your lists automatically.

Table style options

Add Total and Header Rows

What do the new drop-down menu buttons at the top do? Adding a 'Total Row' is an easy way to add up columns.

1 Change the order of the Fruit table to 'Price: Lowest to Highest'.

2 Under **Table Tools**, click **Design**.

3 Tick the 'Total Row' checkbox on the **Table Tools–Design** tab.
A new row is added at the bottom of the table and the final column is added up.

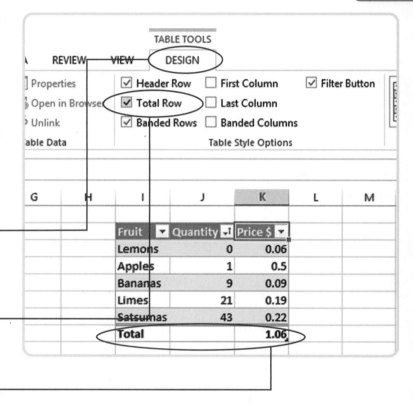

4 Click on the **Total** cell for the *Price* column. A drop-down menu button appears. Click the button to view the options.

5 Select **Sum** to get the total for the column, or **Average** to get the average for the column.

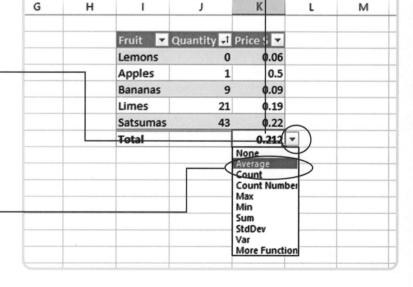

How it looks on paper

Using Print Preview

'Print Preview' lets you check your work before you print it.

1 Create a spreadsheet named *Vacation Plans*. Make a table starting in cell **C5** with three wide columns, 15 tall rows and a title. Apply a 'Table Style' to the cells.

2 Click on the **File** tab and then the **Print** option.

3 Two new areas are displayed; the **Print** area and the **Print Preview** area.

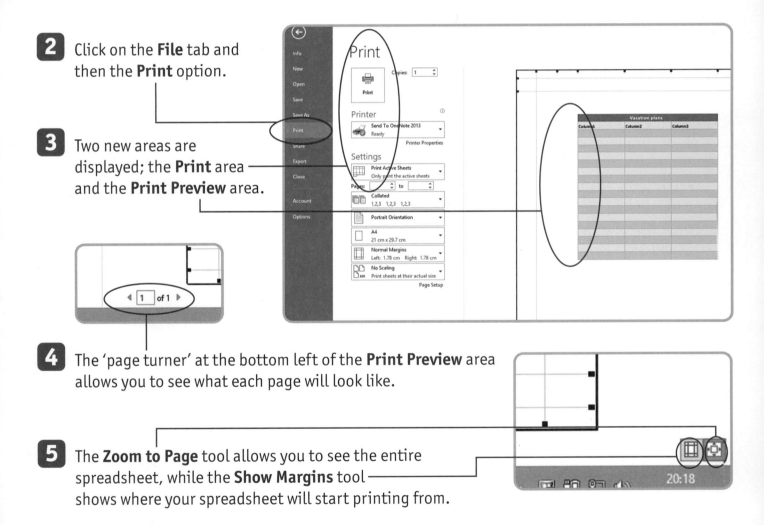

4 The 'page turner' at the bottom left of the **Print Preview** area allows you to see what each page will look like.

5 The **Zoom to Page** tool allows you to see the entire spreadsheet, while the **Show Margins** tool shows where your spreadsheet will start printing from.

6 Press **Esc** to return to the normal view. Notice the dotted lines now on screen. These outline each printed page.

Print part of your work

The Print Area tool

Excel will print everything from cell A1 to the last row and last column where you have edited a cell. To print just a part of your spreadsheet you need to set the 'Print Area'.

1 Select the part of your work that you want to print.

2 Click the **Page Layout** tab on the ribbon and then select the **Print Area** button.

3 From the drop-down menu, select **Set Print Area**.

4 A dotted line appears around your selection and inside, if your **Print Area** will print on more than one page.

5 When the **Print Area** is set, the **Add to Print Area** option appears in the drop-down menu, allowing you to print more areas at the same time.

6 Click on **Clear Print Area** to return to printing the entire spreadsheet.

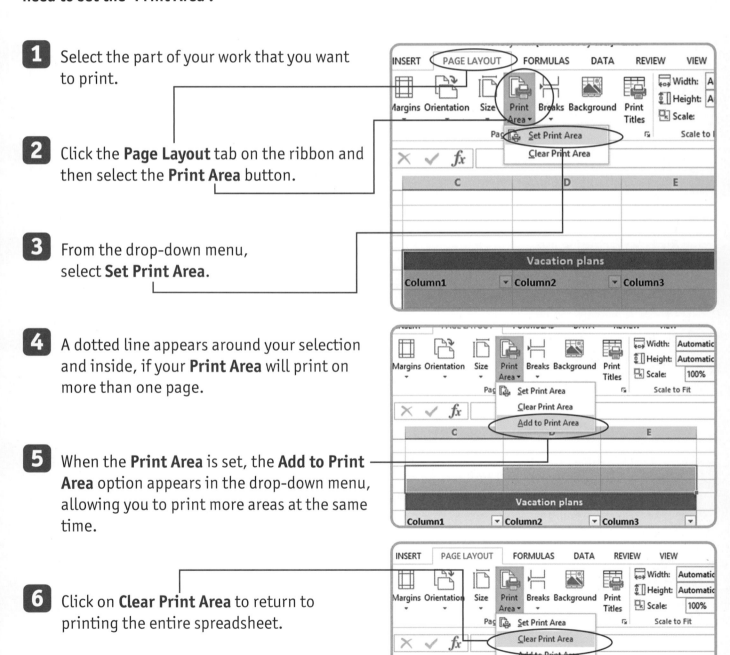

Long or wide

You can print with your paper Landscape or Portrait

Tables can often be wider than they are tall and so are better printed as 'Landscape' rather than the default of 'Portrait'.

1 Make your *Holiday Plan* table much wider. Go to the **Print** area on the **File** tab.

2 In the 'Settings' section, you will see the 'Orientation' setting currently set to **Portrait Orientation**.

3 Click on the menu drop-down button to see and select the **Landscape Orientation** option.

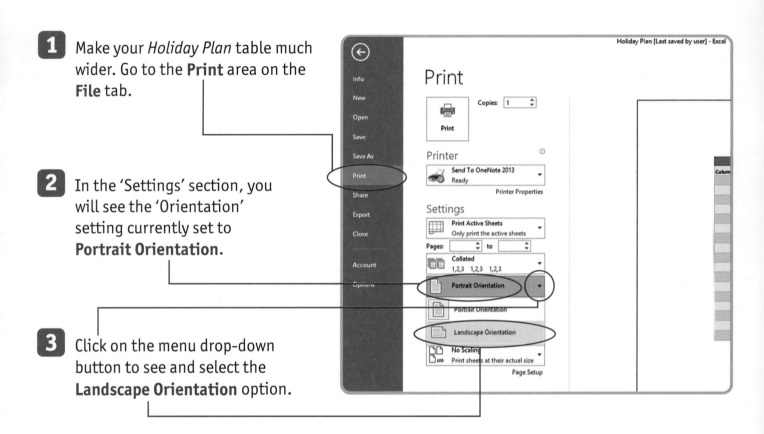

4 The **Print Preview** area will be updated to show the new layout.

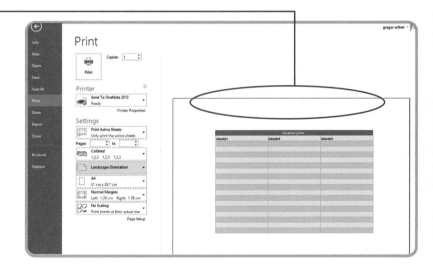

Top Tip!

A painting of a *landscape* is usually wider than it is tall, whereas a *portrait* tends to be taller than it is wide.

Revision plan project

Get ready to print your plan

What will your plan look like on paper? Set the print area for your plan. Change the orientation setting to preview in 'Landscape'.

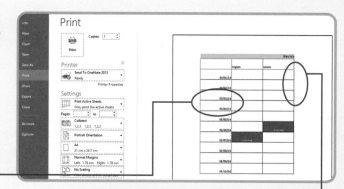

1 Open *Revision Timetable* and set the table row height to *40* and the column width to *20*.

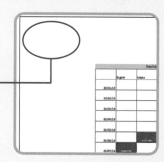

2 Open it in the **Print Preview** area. It won't fit the page.

3 Change column and row sizes until it fits on one page. Preview as you do this to check progress.

4 Insert four rows above and left of the table. Go to the 'Print Preview' area and note how much space is not used.

5 Set the print area to cover the entire plan and preview it again. The margins are now smaller (standard).

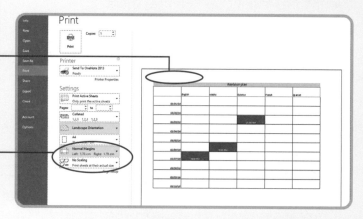

6 Set the column width back to *20* and click **Landscape**. Check the result in the **Print Preview** area. Is it better?

Tools for better printing

Use the Scaling settings to make
your spreadsheet fit your paper.

**You can manually change your spreadsheet to fit,
or you can use scaling settings.**

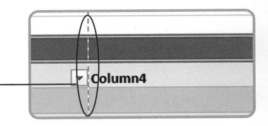

1 Add a column to your *Vacation Plans* table. A dotted line
shows the new column outside your print page area.

2 In the **Print** area the normal
scaling is 'No Scaling'.
Your new column doesn't fit
in the preview.

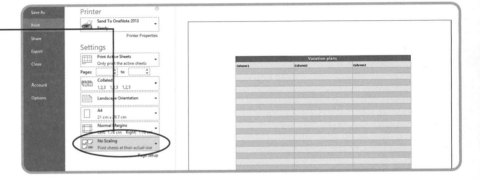

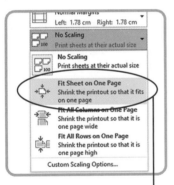

3 Select **Fit Sheet on One Page** if you
want your spreadsheet on just one sheet
of paper.

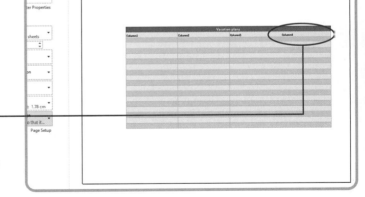

4 The **Print Preview** area will allow you to see
if the scaling has made your work readable.

Top Tip!

In the scaling menu, try **Fit All Columns on One Page**, or **Fit All Rows on One Page**.
You might need to change the orientation if you use these options.

Print your document

The Print and Quick Print buttons

Once you are sure your spreadsheet is ready, go ahead and print.

1 If you want to print more than one copy, type in the number of copies, or click on the **Up Arrow** until you get the right number.

2 Click on the **Print** button to print your work.

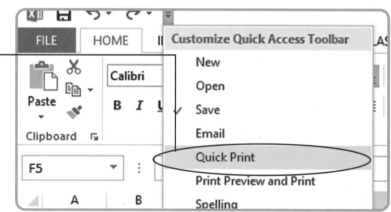

3 For fast printing add the **Quick Print** option to the 'Quick Access' toolbar by selecting it from the drop-down menu.

4 You can then print a single copy by clicking on the new **Quick Print** button in the 'Quick Access' tool-bar.

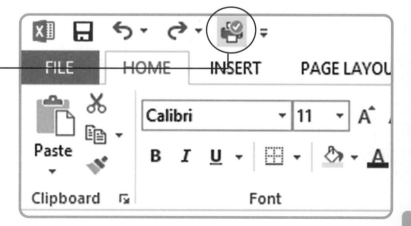

Copy and paste

Repeat something without having to retype it

You often need to copy things again and again on spreadsheets.

1 Select the cells you want to copy. Click the **Copy** button on the **Home** tab. The cells have a moving dotted border.

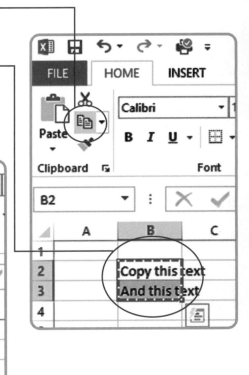

2 Click the cell you want to copy into. If you have copied two or more cells, this will become the top left cell of the range.

3 Click the **Paste** button. A copy appears in the cell you selected.

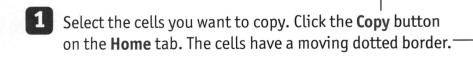

4 To copy again, select another cell and again click **Paste**. You can repeat pasting as long as the 'source' cell(s) are still highlighted.

5 You can paste a single cell into multiple other cells. Each one is filled with a copy when you click **Paste**.

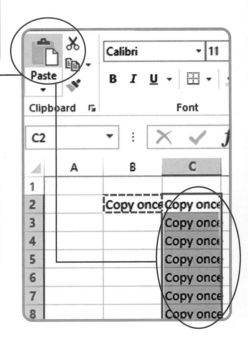

Moving

Move things around the spreadsheet

Moving or cutting and pasting content helps you reorganize your work.

1 Select the cells you want to move. The cells have a moving dotted border. Click the **Cut** button on the **Home** tab.

2 Click on the cell the cut cells will move to.

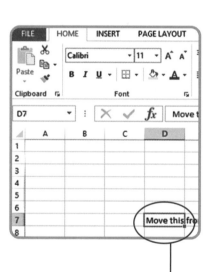

3 Click the **Paste** button. The cut cells appear at the selected cell.

4 To move cells directly, select them and hover-over the edge of the selected area until the mouse pointer changes to crossed arrows.

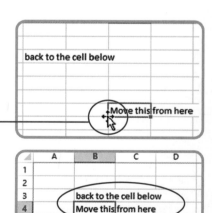

5 Click-and-drag the cells to a new position.

Turn back time

Using the Undo and Redo buttons

You will sometimes make mistakes and need to reverse them.

1 Open a workbook and select a cell. Apply the *Good* style to it.

2 Click the **Undo** button in the **Quick Access** toolbar. The style will disappear. Type the numbers *1* to *6* in column **C**.

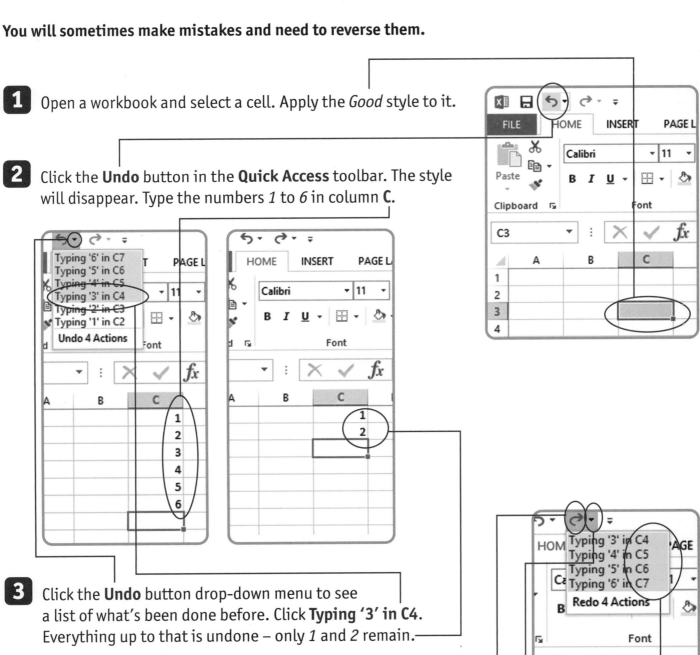

3 Click the **Undo** button drop-down menu to see a list of what's been done before. Click **Typing '3' in C4**. Everything up to that is undone – only *1* and *2* remain.

4 If you have undone too much, click the **Redo** button until you get back to where you want, or click the drop-down menu and select the actions you want to redo.

My diary project

Create a diary

Use copy and paste to build up a large spreadsheet. Use cut and paste to rearrange things. Use Undo to reverse your changes.

1 Save a new spreadsheet as *My Diary*. In cell **C5** start a table with days of the month to 31 across the top and times of day down the side. Style it.

2 Select your table and click **Copy**. Select a blank cell in column **C** and click **Paste**. Repeat until you have 12 tables.

3 Select the first row of the diary. Cut and paste it into cell **A3**. Select the other rows and cut and paste them below the first one.

4 Select the next table and click-and-drag it to column **A**. Move all the remaining tables to column **A**.

5 Undo the pastes that moved the table from its original position.

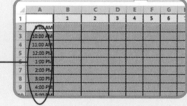

6 Redo the pastes to get the tables back to their positions starting in cell **A3**.

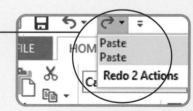

The history of copying

Using the Clipboard

Every time you 'copy' or 'cut' something, it is added to the Clipboard for reuse.

1 Click the **Clipboard** toolset drop-down menu on the **Home** tab.

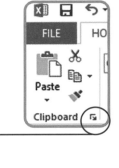

2 The **Clipboard** appears showing recently copied 'Clips'.

Top Tip!

The 'Clipboard' holds information from other programs too. Great if you are copying from a **Word** document!

3 To reuse a 'Clip', select a cell then select the 'Clip' you want on the
Clipboard. It is pasted into your selected cell(s).

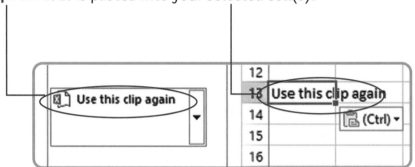

4 The **Clipboard** can hold lots of 'Clips'. New 'Clips' replace old ones.
To keep an old 'Clip', delete some newer ones.
Hover-over a 'Clip', click its drop-down menu button and select **Delete**.

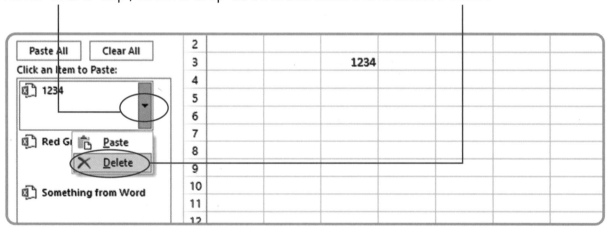

5 To close the **Clipboard**, click the **Close** button
in the top-right corner.

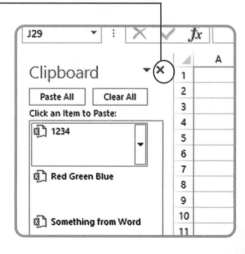

5 Speed it up

Copy just the value

Copy, but keep the format of where you are pasting

The Paste button drop-down menu has several useful options. Paste Values allows you to paste the content of a cell without its style.

1 Type the words shown here into cells as shown. Give two cells a yellow background, a 14pt blue font and red dotted border. ———— Make the backgrounds of the other two green and the font 20pt *Arial Black*. ————

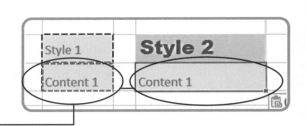

2 Copy a *Style 1* cell. Select the empty *Style 2* cell. Using the **Paste** button gives it a *Style 1* style. The style is copied as well.

3 To avoid this, click the **Paste** button drop-down menu. ————

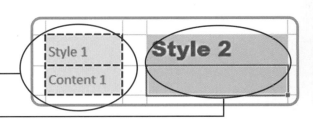

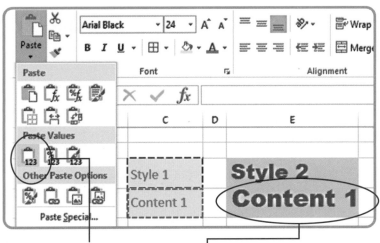

4 Select **Paste Values.** The text only has now been pasted, not the style.

My diary project

Add features to the diary

Use the Clipboard for speed, and Paste Values to keep the table style.

1 On a new worksheet, create a list of the 12 months. Style with *Heading 2*. Open the Clipboard and copy each month, one at a time.

2 On the Diary Worksheet, insert a new column in **A**. Select a cell and click a month on the Clipboard.

3 Set the Diary table text to *9pt* with **Wrap Text**. Create a list of special events on another worksheet. Open the Clipboard and copy each event, one at a time.

4 Use the **Paste Values** option to keep the text wrapped at *9pt*.

5 Click on the special event cell and add background color. Use the **Format Painter** (see next page) to color the whole day. Then use it for the other special days.

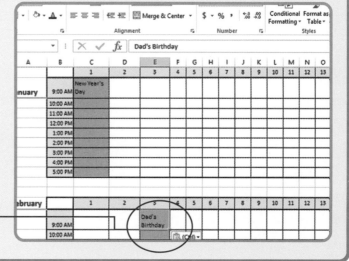

Copy just the style

The Format Painter

Sometimes you want to copy just the style of a cell, not the content.

1 Click on the cell whose style you want to copy.

2 Click the **Format Painter** button from the 'Clipboard' toolset.

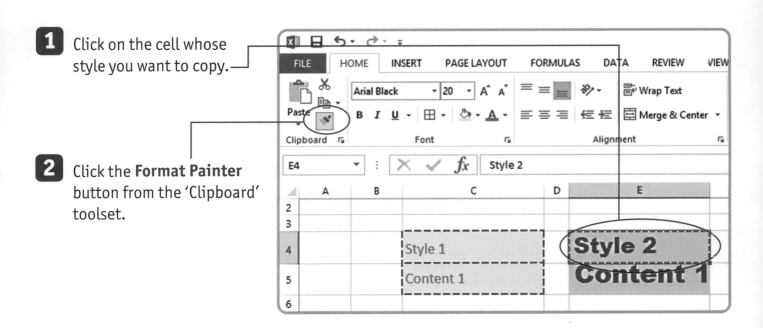

3 The mouse pointer will change to a paintbrush icon to show that the 'Format Painter' is active.

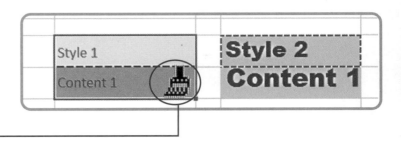

4 Click or click-and-drag over the cells you want to apply this styling to. This paints the cell style only into the cells you have activated.

5 The 'Format Painter' is only available once. Click back on the source cell and repeat to use it again.

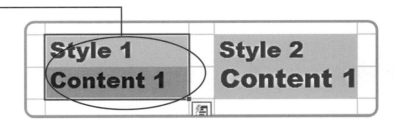

Linking together

Using Hyperlink to help get about

You can use hyperlinks to move quickly around a spreadsheet.

1 Type *Jump to here* in a cell on a worksheet and *Click here* in another cell.

2 Select the *Jump to here* cell. In the 'Name Box', type *Link1*. (Names can't have spaces in them.)

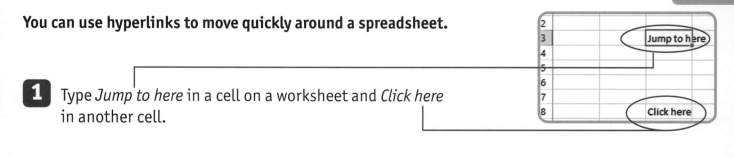

3 Click on the *Click here* (link) cell. Click the **Hyperlink** button on the **Insert** tab. The 'Insert Hyperlink' dialog box appears.

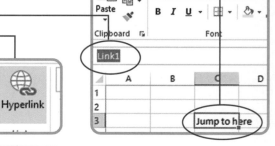

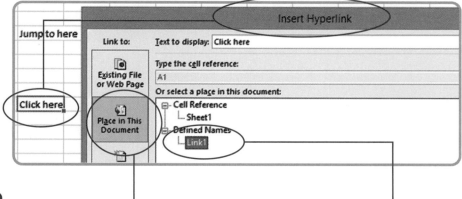

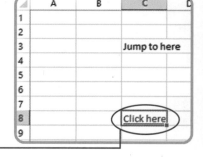

4 Click the **Place in This Document** button and select *Link1* from the 'Defined Names' list. Click **OK**. The cell style changes to *Hyperlink*.

5 Clicking on the linked cell will move you to the *Jump to here* cell. Right-clicking on the *Click here* cell will let you select the **Remove Hyperlink** option.

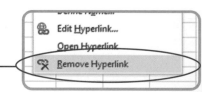

Check your text

Using the Spellchecker and Thesaurus

Excel can check spellings and help with language.

1 To check your spelling, click the **Spelling** button on the **Review** tab.

2 If it finds a query the 'Spelling' dialog box appears, with the problem word in the 'Not in Dictionary' field.

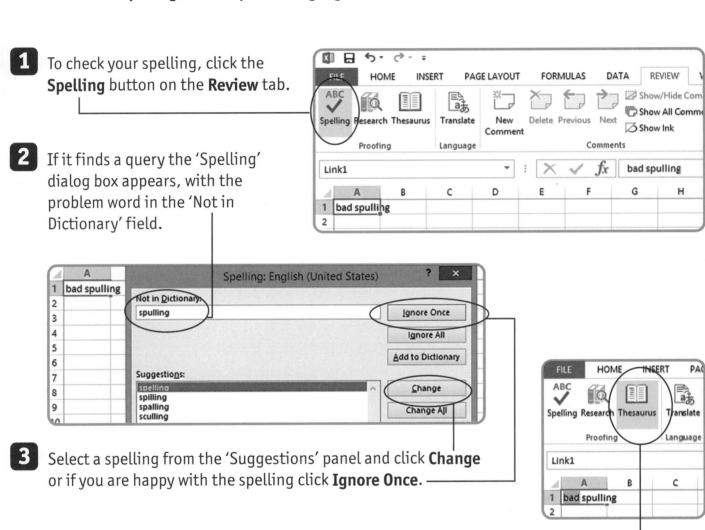

3 Select a spelling from the 'Suggestions' panel and click **Change** or if you are happy with the spelling click **Ignore Once**.

4 To use the thesaurus, click the **Thesaurus** button. A 'Pane' appears on the right of the screen with suggestions about a selected word.

5 If nothing is selected on the spreadsheet, type a word in the 'Search for' field and click the **Blue Arrow** button.

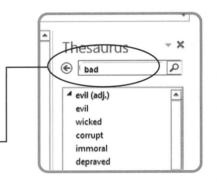

My diary project

Get around the diary and check

Use Hyperlinks for speed, check spelling and try different words.

1 Select each month cell in the *My Diary* worksheet and name it.

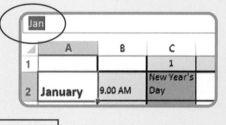

2 Go to the other worksheet and select *January*. Add a hyperlink to the defined name *Jan*.

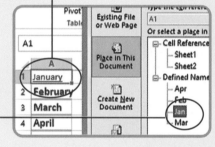

3 Repeat for the other months. Click on a link to take you to that month.

4 Notice that links change color once used. This is automatic in **Excel**.

5 Select cell **A1** and click the **Spelling** button.

6 Correct any errors.

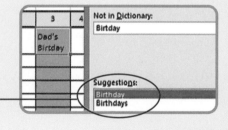

7 Click the **Thesaurus** button.
Find a new word for *Birthday*.

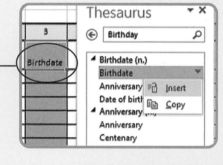

8 Save and close the *My Diary* spreadsheet.

Simple sums

Simple calculations in a cell

Excel is designed to do number crunching from simple to very difficult.

Top Tip!

If you want to combine adding and subtracting with multiplication and division, you need to use <u>brackets</u>. Calculations in brackets are done first. So (2+2)x3=12 but 2+(2x3)=8.

1 Any calculation in **Excel** begins with =. This tells **Excel** the cell contains a calculation, not text.

2 To add two numbers, click in a cell and type *=10+10*. Then press the **Enter** key.

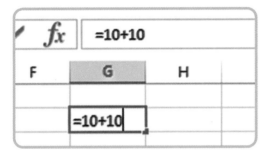

fx	=10+10			*fx*	=10+10
F	**G**	H		F	**G**	H
	=10+10				20

3 The answer, *20*, is shown in the cell, while the calculation is shown in the formula bar.

4 To subtract, use the – key. Multiply is * and divide is /.

fx	=20-10		*fx*	=10*10		*fx*	=20/10
F	**G**	H	F	**G**	H	F	**G**	H
	10			100			2

Start the power

Simple calculations between cells

You can also do calculations on the numbers in cells. For example, you can add up the contents of five cells and put the answer in a sixth cell.

1 Open a new spreadsheet and name it *Calculation*.

2 Type the numbers *43, 56, 345, 67* and *65* into cells **D2** to **D6**. We will now add these up and put the answer in cell **D7**.

	A	B	C	D	E
1					
2				43	
3				56	
4				345	
5				67	
6				65	
7				=D2	

3 In cell **D7** (our answer cell) type =. Then click on cell **D2** containing the first number. *D2* appears (not the number inside it) meaning the calculation will be done using the number contained in cell **D2**.

	A	B	C	D	E
1					
2				43	
3				56	
4				345	
5				67	
6				65	
7				=D2+D3+D4+D5+D6	

4 Press the + key and then click the next cell. Repeat for all the cells with numbers. Cell **D7** will show=*D2+D3+D4+D5+D6*.

Continued on the next page

5 Press the **Enter** key to tell **Excel** the calculation is complete. The answer cell **D7** now shows the result of adding the contents of the five cells together (*576*).

	A	B	C	D	E
1					
2				43	
3				56	
4				345	
5				67	
6				65	
7				576	
8					
9					

6 Change the number in **D3** from *56* to *0*. Notice the number in the answer cell has changed to *520*. The calculation is updated automatically.

	A	B	C	D	E
1					
2				43	
3				0	
4				345	
5				67	
6				65	
7				520	

Top Tip!

You can create calculations before putting numbers in the cells you refer to.

Top Tip!

The column letter and row number of a cell is called the **Cell Reference**. Cell **A1** is the top left cell of a worksheet.

Class survey project

Starting your class survey

Learn to use Excel for simple calculations first.

1 Create a spreadsheet *Class Survey*. Add the class's names to column **A**.
In cells **B3** to **E3** type *Cats*, *Dogs*, *Other* and *Total*. Add a title *Number of Pets*.

2			Number of Pets		
3	Name	Cats	Dogs	Other	Total
4	Michael	1	2	3	=1+2+3
5	Felix	2	0	1	
6	Sophie	0	1	0	
7	Ali		0	1	
8	Kinga	0	2	0	
9					

2 Fill in the 'Number of Pets' columns. In cell **E4** add up the number of pets that Michael has. Press **Enter**.

2			Number of Pets		
3	Name	Cats	Dogs	Other	Total
4	Michael	1	2	3	6
5	Felix	2	0	1	=B5+C5+D5
6	Sophie	0	1	0	
7	Ali	3	0	1	
8	Kinga	0	2	0	
9					

3 Using the cell references in row 5, set up the calculation for Felix's total number of pets in cell **E5**.

4 Do the same for the other 'Total' cells.

2			Number of Pets		
3	Name	Cats	Dogs	Other	Total
4	Michael	1	2	3	6
5	Felix	2	0	1	3
6	Sophie	0	1	0	1
7	Ali	3	0	1	4
8	Kinga	0	2	0	2
9					

Build up steam

Copying formulas

Fill a spreadsheet with sums. It's easy when you learn how to copy calculations.

1 Create two columns each containing numbers *1* to *10*.

2 Create a formula (a sum type) to multiply the first two numbers together.

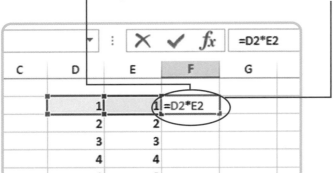

	:	✕ ✓ *fx*	=D2*E2

C	D	E	F	G
	1	1	=D2*E2	
	2	2		
	3	3		
	4	4		
	5	5		

	:	✕ ✓ *fx*	=D2*E2

C	D	E	F	G
	1	1	1	
	2	2		
	3	3		
	4	4		
	5	5		

3 Copy the cell with the calculation and paste it into the cells below.
Excel automatically adjusts the cell names. See how the first row shows
=D2*E2. **Excel** has adjusted the next row so the calculation is *=D3*E3*.

	:	✕ ✓ *fx*	

C	D	E	F	G
	1	1	1	
	2	2		
	3	3		
	4	4		
	5	5		
	6	6		
	7	7		
	8	8		
	9	9		
	10	10		

	:	✕ ✓ *fx*	=D3*E3

C	D	E	F	G
	1	1	1	
	2	2	4	
	3	3	9	
	4	4	16	
	5	5	25	
	6	6	36	
	7	7	49	
	8	8	64	
	9	9	81	
	10	10	100	

4 Sometimes you want to copy cells without this happening. In this example, we want to see how many apples we can buy for $3.

	Apples	Price of one apple
	1	0.33
	2	
	3	
	4	
	5	
	6	
	7	
	8	
	9	
	10	

C	D	E
	Apples	Price of one apple
	1	0.33
	2	=D3*E2
	3	

5 If we create the formula in cell **E3** and copy to cell **E4** it becomes =D4*E3 with a wrong result of *1.98*–it should be *0.99*.

	D	E	F
	Apples	Price of one apple	
	1	0.33	
	2	0.66	
	3	1.98	
	4		

6 To tell **Excel** to copy a formula <u>without</u> the cell reference (cell name) being changed, add the *$* symbol to the column and/or row reference. To get the price of 3 to 10 apples right, change the formula in cell **D4** to =D3*E$2. Then copy to the other cells.

Apples	Price of one apple
1	0.33
2	0.66
3	0.99
4	1.32
5	1.65
6	1.98
7	2.31
8	2.64
9	=D10*E$2
10	3.3

Apples	Price of one apple
1	0.33
2	0.66
3	0.99
4	1.32
5	1.65
6	1.98
7	2.31
8	2.64
9	2.97
10	3.3

7 Now you can see all the sums in column **E**, use the price of one apple in cell **E2**. We can buy 9 apples for $3, with 3 cents change.

Total power

Adding up using **AutoSum**

Excel can add cells together easily using 'AutoSum'. This adds the numbers in selected cells together and puts the answer in a cell.

1 Copy the table. Click on cell **C8** in the 'Total' row. Click the **AutoSum** button on the **Home** tab.

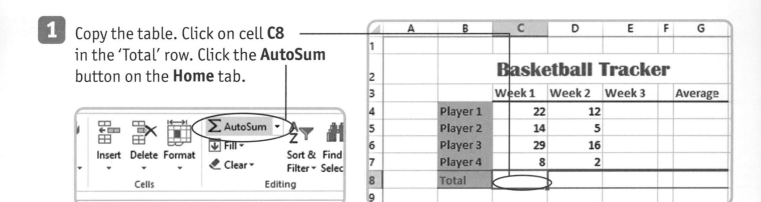

	Week 1	Week 2	Week 3	Average
Basketball Tracker				
Player 1	22	12		
Player 2	14	5		
Player 3	29	16		
Player 4	8	2		
Total				

2 'AutoSum' guesses what cells you want to add together. Press **Enter** if the right cells are selected, or select the right cells and press the **Enter** key.
The total of all the cells appears in **C8**.

3 To find the average score for *Player 1*, use the options in the **AutoSum** button drop-down menu. Click on cell **G4**. Select **Average**.

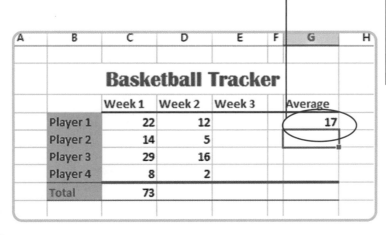

	Week 1	Week 2	Week 3	Average
Basketball Tracker				
Player 1	22	12		17
Player 2	14	5		
Player 3	29	16		
Player 4	8	2		
Total	73			

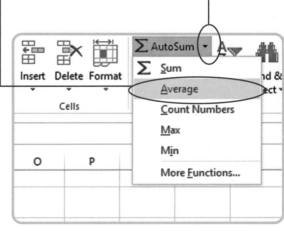

Class survey project

Speed through your class survey

Complete the survey by copying the formulas and using AutoSum.

1 Add a new column 'Cost of cats' in **F2** with the cost of a cat in **F3** as *17*. Create the formula in **F4**, which will refer to cell **F3** when copied, using the $ key.

	Number of Pets			Cost of cats
Cats	Dogs	Other	Total	17
1	2	3	6	=B4*F$3
2	0	1	3	

2 Copy **F4** and paste into the cells below.

	Number of Pets			Cost of cats
Cats	Dogs	Other	Total	17
1	2	3	6	17
2	0	1	3	34
0	1	0	1	0
3	0	1	4	51
0	2	0	2	0

3 Type *Total* below the names in column **A**. Add up the number of cats using **AutoSum** in cell **B9**.

3	Name	Cats	Dogs	Other	Total
4	Michael	1	2	3	6
5	Felix	2	0	1	3
6	Sophie	0	1	0	1
7	Ali	3	0	1	4
8	Kinga	0	2	0	2
9	Total	=SUM(B4:B8)			
10		SUM(number1, [number2],)			

4 Using click-and-drag autofill, copy and paste the *Total* sum across the row to get the totals of each column.

2		Number of Pets			
3	Name	Cats	Dogs	Other	Total
4	Michael	1	2	3	6
5	Felix	2	0	1	3
6	Sophie	0	1	0	1
7	Ali	3	0	1	4
8	Kinga	0	2	0	2
9	Total	6	5	5	16

5 Type *Average* in **D10**. Using the 'Average' option in **AutoSum**, find the average number of pets each friend has. Make sure you drag the selection box up so the total is not included.

Name	Cats	Dogs	Other	Total
Michael	1	2	3	6
Felix	2	0	1	3
Sophie	0	1	0	1
Ali	3	0	1	4
Kinga	0	2	0	2
Total	6	5	5	16
			Average	=AVERAGE(E4:E

Formulas and functions

Inserting Functions into a spreadsheet

Excel can use clever functions to produce an answer from the numbers you put in.

1 We can show if a player's score is above or below a team average.

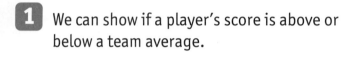

	Week 1	Week 2	Week 2 Ave	Week
Player 1	22	12		
Player 2	14	5		
Player 3	29	16		
Player 4	8	2		
Total	73	35	=AVERAGE(D4:D7)	

2 Insert a new column in front of column **E**. Name it *Week 2 Ave*.
In cell **E8** calculate the average for Week 2.
The formula is (=AVERAGE(D4:D7).

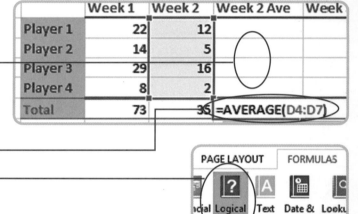

3 Click on cell **E4**, then click the **Logical Function** button on the **Formulas** tab and select the **IF** option.
The 'Function Arguments' dialog box opens.

4 Write *D4>E$8* in the **Logical_test** field,

"*Above*" in the **Value_if_true** field,

"*Below*" in the **Value_if_false** field.

Function Arguments

Logical_test	D4>E$8
Value_if_true	"Above"
Value_if_false	Below

This asks **Excel** 'Is *Player 1*'s score higher than average?' Click **OK**.

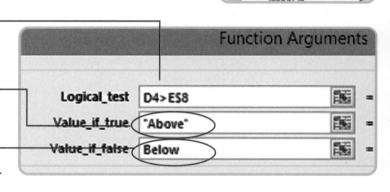

Basketball Tracker

	Week 1	Week 2	Week 2 Ave	Week 3
Player 1	22	12	Above	
Player 2	14	5	Below	
Player 3	29	16	Above	
Player 4	8	2	Below	
Total	73	35	8.75	

5 Copy cell **E4** and paste into the cells below. **Excel** tells you who scored *Above* and *Below* the average for that week.

Number and number

Other number formats: Decimals

Excel normally displays up to 9 decimal places, but you can increase, reduce or fix it.

1 If you calculate 1/3, **Excel** displays this as 0.333333333. You don't always want to show all the decimals.

2 Click the **Decrease Decimal** button on the **Home** tab to reduce them.

3 Click the **Increase Decimal** button to increase the decimals shown.

4 Click the **Number Format** button to set the number of decimal places.

5 Set the number of decimal places in the 'Format Cells' dialog box that appears.

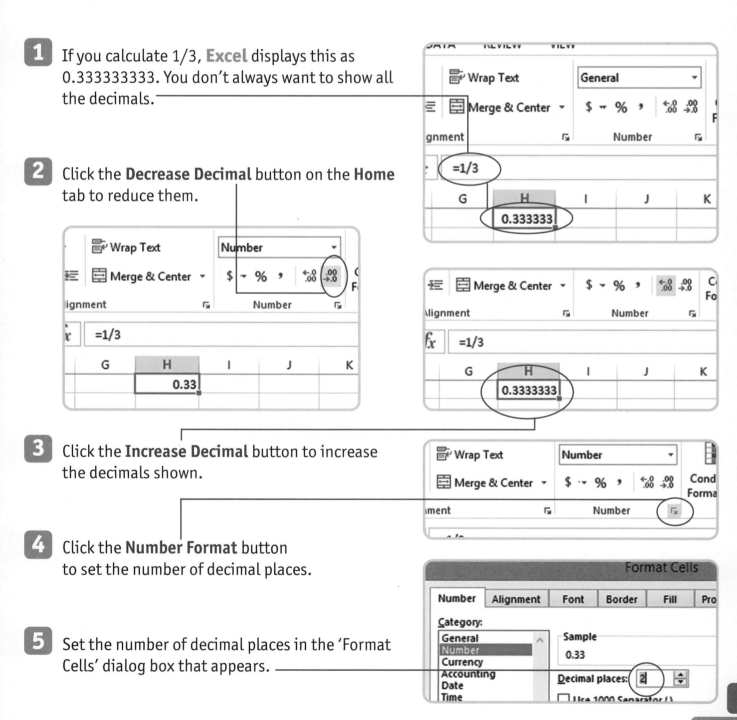

Number and number

Other number formats: Currencies, Percentages and 1000s

Number formats can display numbers as money and percentages, and separate thousands with commas.

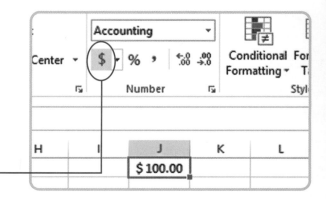

1 Show the number in a cell as currency by clicking the **Accounting Number Format** button.

2 To use another currency symbol, click the **Accounting Number Format** button drop-down menu and select one, e.g. **£ English (United Kindom)**.

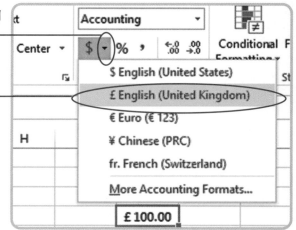

3 To show numbers as a percentage where 100% = 1 (so *4/7* appears as *57%* and *3.5* as *350%*) click the **Percent Style** button.

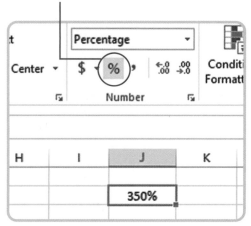

4 To show numbers with a comma in the 1000s, for example 30,000 not 30000, click the **Comma Style** button. This is a special accounting style that also fixes the cell to 2 decimal places.

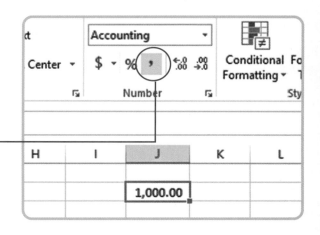

Class survey project

Tidy up the survey

The average number of pets was 3.2! Sort the table numbers into units and money, then ask **Excel** which pet rules.

C	D	E	F	G
Number of Pets			Cost of cats	
Dogs	Other	Total	$ 17.00	
2	3	6	$ 17.00	
0	1	3	$ 34.00	
1	0	1	$ -	
0	1	4	$ 51.00	
2	0	2	$ -	
5	5	16	$ 102.00	
	Average	3	$ 20.40	

1 Click the **Decrease Decimal** button on the **Home** tab to remove the *0.2* of a pet.

2 Select the *Cost of cats* column and set the **Number Format** menu to **Accounting**.

3 We want **Excel** to decide which pet rules. Type *which pet rules* in **G2**.

	Number of Pets				Cost of cats	which pet rules	
	Cats	Dogs	Other	Total	$ 17.00		
el	1	2	3	6	$ 17.00		
	2	0	1	3	$ 34.00		
e	0	1	0	1	$ -		
	3	0	1	4	$ 51.00		
	0	2	0	2	$ -		
	6	5	5	16	$ 102.00	(s Rule)	
			Average	3	$ 20.40		

IF

Logical_test B9>C9
Value_if_true Cats rule
Value_if_false Dogs Rule

4 Click cell **G9**. Press the **Logical** button and select **IF**.

5 Click on the **Logical_test** field, click on the *Cats Total* cell **B9** then type >. Then click on the *Dogs Total* cell **C9**.

6 In the **Value_if_true** field type *Cats rule*. In the **Value_if_false** field type *Dogs rule* and click **OK**.

Excel says cats are more popular.

	0	1	4	$ 51.00	
	2	0	2	$ -	
	5	5	16	$ 102.00	Cats rule
		Average	3	$ 20.40	

Setting a date

Date and time formats

There are many ways of showing dates and times. For example, you can write 6/12/11 or Sunday, June 12, 2011. **Excel** even lets you make up your own way.

1 The formula *=Now()* gives the current date and time. Use this in a cell.

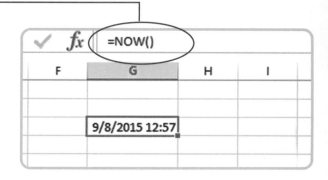

2 On the **Home** tab, use the **Number Format** button drop-down menu options. **Short Date** displays the date but no time.

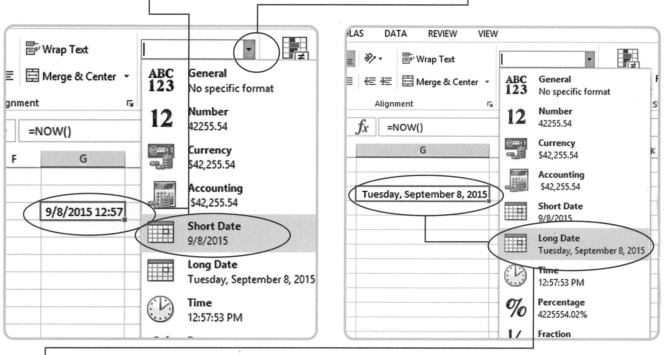

3 **Long Date** displays the month as a word–*April,* not *04/*.

4 The **Time** option shows just the time.

5 To use other date and time options, click the **Format Button** in the 'Cells' toolset.

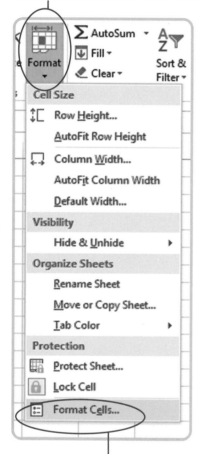

6 Select the **Format Cells** and a dialog box appears. Select **Date** or **Time** and then the format type you want. The 'Sample' panel shows how it will look on screen.

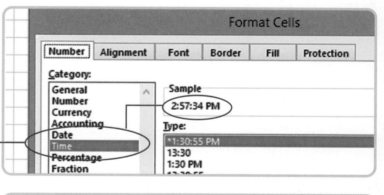

7 If you cannot find the format you want, click on **Custom** in the 'Category' panel. There are more options there.

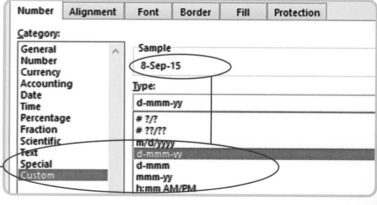

Visualize your data

Create a basic column Chart

One of Excel's strengths is how easily it can convert information into charts and graphs.

Average Temperatures °F		
Month	Max	Min
January	64	46
February	64	48
March	66	48
April	70	50
May	72	54
June	75	55
July	81	61
August	82	61
September	81	57
October	75	54
November	73	50
December	66	46

1 Open a new spreadsheet named *Graphs* and make up a temperature table. Select the data to turn into a graph, including headings.

2 On the **Insert** tab, click the **Column** chart button drop-down menu.

3 Select a type of column chart.

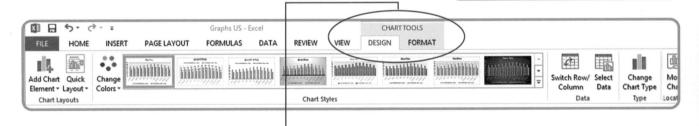

4 A chart appears along with the **Chart Tools** Ribbon tabset. **Excel** uses the first column for the horizontal axis and treats all other columns as data.

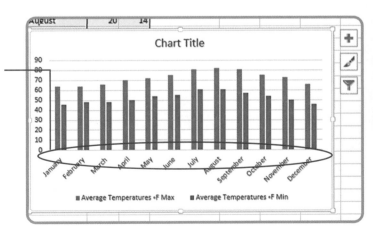

Design your chart

Other ways of looking at it

There are lots of options to adjust the look of charts in the Design tab of the Chart Tools Ribbon tabset.

1 To move your chart to another worksheet, click the **Move Chart** button.

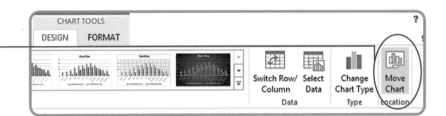

2 The 'Move Chart' dialog box appears. Choose a worksheet or make a new worksheet. Select the **New Sheet** option, name it *Temperature Chart* and click **OK**.

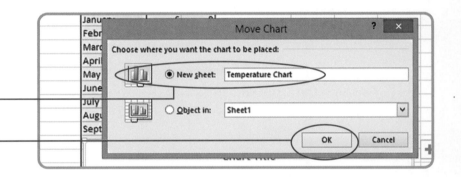

3 A new worksheet called *Temperature Chart* has been created with your chart on it.

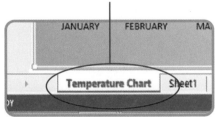

4 For column colors and effects, select from the 'Chart Styles' toolset on the **Design** tab. Click the toolset drop-down menu to view options.

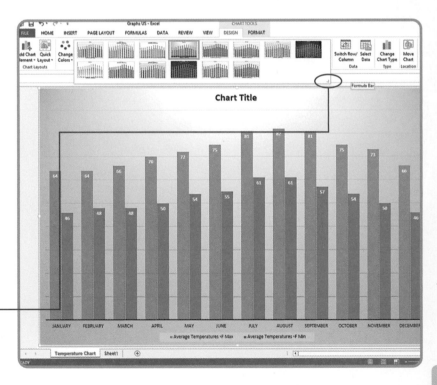

What are you looking at?

Lay out your column chart

The Design tab on the Chart Tools Ribbon tabset has all the options needed to label charts.

1 To add a chart title, click the **Add Chart Element** drop-down menu button. Select the title option you want to use.

2 Double-click into the title box to edit the title.

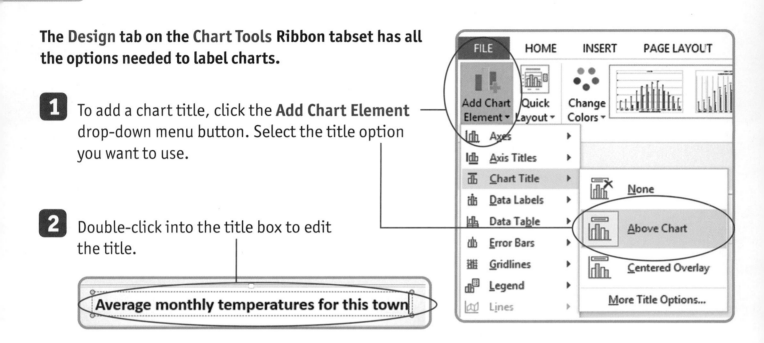

3 The **Axis Titles** button labels the axes. Here we have a vertical axis label.

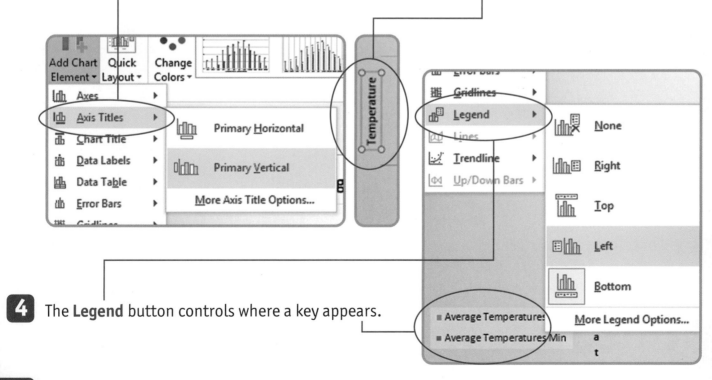

4 The **Legend** button controls where a key appears.

Class presentation project

Create a pet ownership chart

Use the *Class survey* spreadsheet to create a chart using tools learnt.

1 Open your *Class survey* spreadsheet. Select the *Name*, *Cats*, *Dogs* and *Other* columns.

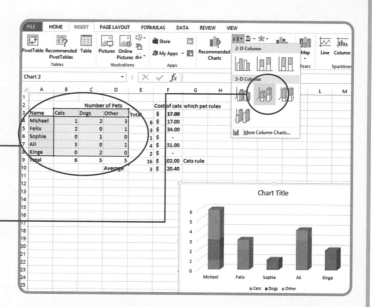

2 Choose a 'stacked cylinder' column chart to go beside your table.

3 Select the whole table then sort the data by the *Total* column. Deselect the Total column.

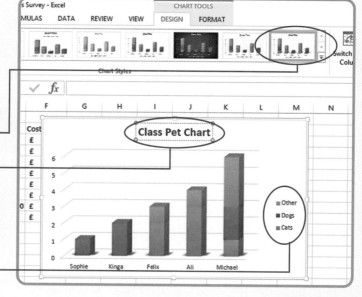

4 Notice that the chart changes as the data is sorted.

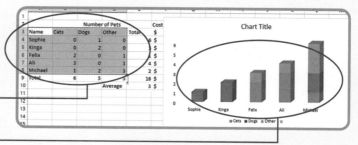

5 Select a style for the chart from the 'Chart Styles' toolset.

6 Add a Chart Title and arrange the chart Legend to the right.

More layout options

The Chart Tools – Design and Format tabs

These layout options can add information and change chart background styles.

1 Click the **Add Chart Element** drop-down menu button and select **Data Labels** to put the actual number a column represents, above or on it.

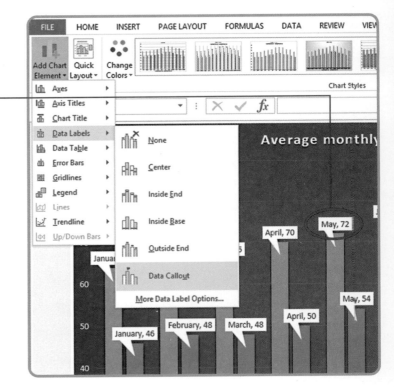

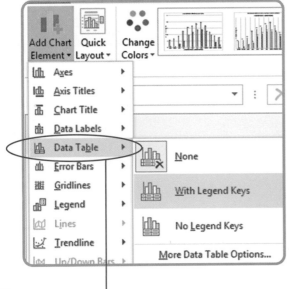

2 The **Data Table** option puts a copy of the source data on the chart; useful when the original is on a different worksheet.

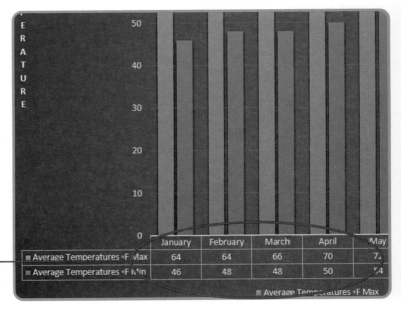

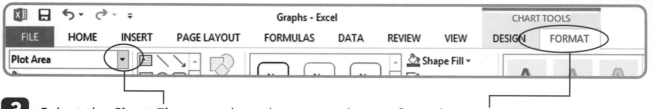

3 Select the **Chart Elements** drop-down menu button from the **Format** tab on the **Chart Tools** Ribbon tabset.

4 Select the **Plot Area** option to change the chart background. For 3-D style charts there are more choices. Select **Side Wall** and a handle appears showing you what can be changed.

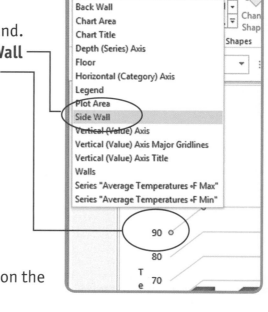

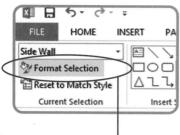

5 Select **Format Selection**. The 'Format Wall' pane appears on the right of your screen.

6 Select **Fill** for options to add color, pictures or other backgrounds. Explore their effects on the selection.

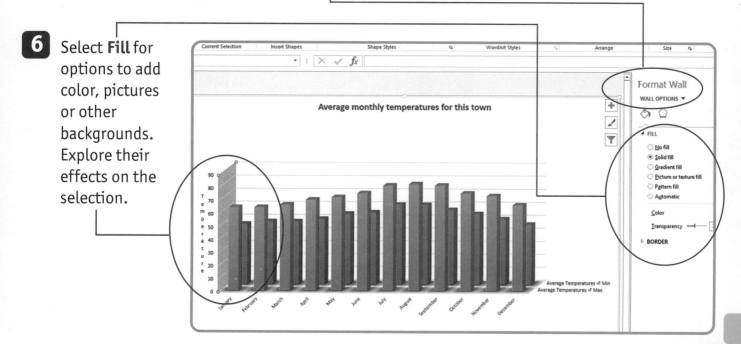

More Format options

The Chart Tools – Format tab

Using the Format tab lets you style the text and background of different parts of your chart.

1 Click the **Format** tab in the **Chart Tools** Ribbon tabset.

2 Select 'Chart Title' from the **Chart Elements** drop-down menu, or click on the chart element you want to style, for example the 'Chart Title'.

3 Select a 'Shape Styles' toolset option to style the shape and background of the 'Chart Title'.

4 Select the 'Vertical Axis Title' from the **Chart Elements** drop-down menu.
To use the 'Format Axis Title' pane, click on the toolset button or apply a style.

Class presentation project

Style your chart

Use the Chart Tools – Design and Format tab options to add styling.

1 Use the **Move Chart** button to create a new bigger chart. Use the **Data Labels** button drop-down menu for column labels.

2 Add a **Data Table** to your chart.

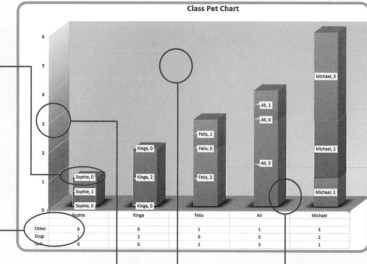

3 In **Format – Chart Elements** menu, select **Side Wall**, **Back Wall** and **Floor**. Create 'Gradient fills' for the background.

4 Click the 'Chart Title' and 'Legend' and apply shape styles. Click-and-drag the corners to make them bigger.

5 Insert 'Vertical Axis'. Apply a 'WordArt' style. Select a reflection option from the **Text Effects** button drop-down menu.

6 On the labels and legend use the **Grow Font** button on the **Home** tab.

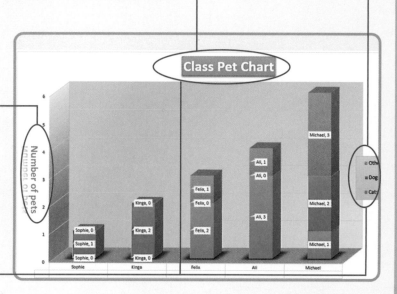

Mmmm, pie (charts)!

Pie charts and other chart styles

Excel can also create Pie, Doughnut, Bar and Line charts. The Design, Layout and Format tab options are similar to column chart ones.

1 Open a new spreadsheet and create this *Favorite Movies* table. Select it.

2 Click the **Pie Chart** button drop-down menu in the 'Charts' toolset on the **Insert** tab. Select the '3-D Pie' option.

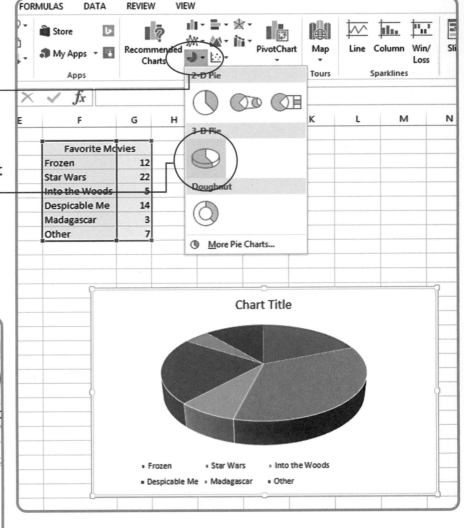

3 Or select a 'Doughnut' chart.

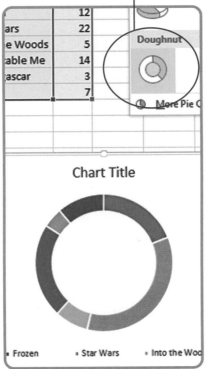

4 Or make your pie chart explode into pieces. Click on your pie chart and select a chart style from the **Chart Tools – Design** Tabset.

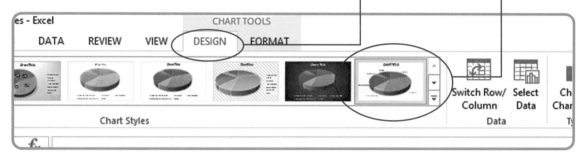

5 Select **Series 1** from the **Chart Elements** drop-down menu in **Chart Tools – Format**.

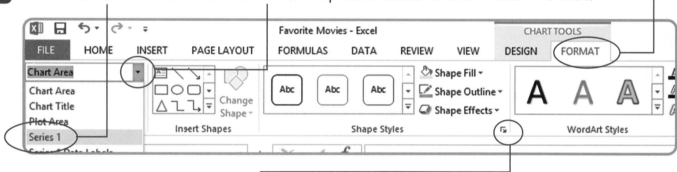

6 Click the 'Shape Styles' toolset button. The 'Format Data Point' pane appears to the right. The pie segments ('Series 1') are already selected. Adjust the **Series Options** sliders to explode the pie.

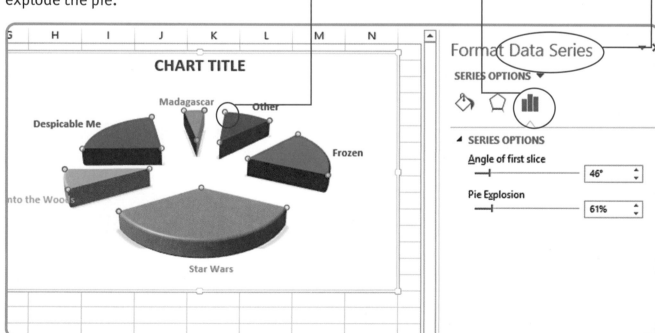

Let Excel decide

Use Recommended Charts to see choices

The Recommended Charts tool lets you quickly see the table turned into the best types of chart.

1 Open the *Basketball* spreadsheet. On the Insert tab, click the **Recommended Charts** button.

| HOME | INSERT | PAGE LAYOUT | FORMULAS | DATA | REVIEW | VIEW |

Recommended PivotTables — Table — Pictures — Online Pictures — Store — My Apps — Recommended Charts

Tables — Illustrations — Apps — Ch

=AVERAGE(D4:D7)

Basketball Tracker

	Week 1	Week 2	Week 2 Ave	Week 3	Average
Player 1	22	12	Above		17
Player 2	14	5	Below		
Player 3	29	16	Above		
Player 4	8	2	Below		
Total	73	35	8.75		

2 The **Insert Chart** box appears. Click to preview in the **Recommended Charts** field and select the chart that makes your information clearest.

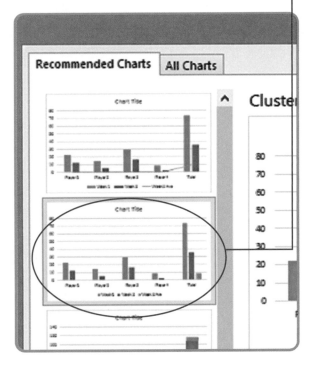

3 Open the *Favorite Movies* spreadsheet. In the **Insert Chart** box, click to preview the **All Charts** field and find a chart that makes your information really striking.

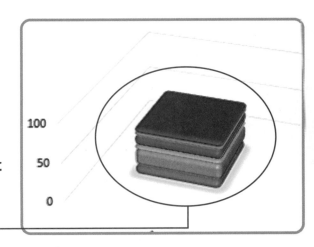

Class presentation project

Time for Pie. Does Excel agree?

Let Excel decide what the best chart type for the survey should be.

1 Click the **Pie Chart** button drop-down menu in the 'Charts' toolset on the **Insert** tab. Select a 'Pie in 2-D' option.

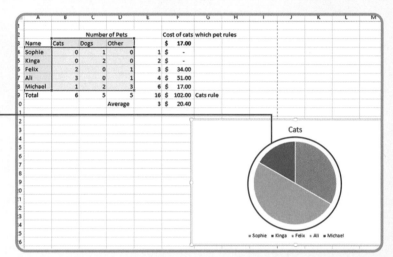

2 Click the **Recommended Charts** button in the 'Charts' toolset on the **Insert** tab. **Excel** does not recommend a pie chart for the class survey.

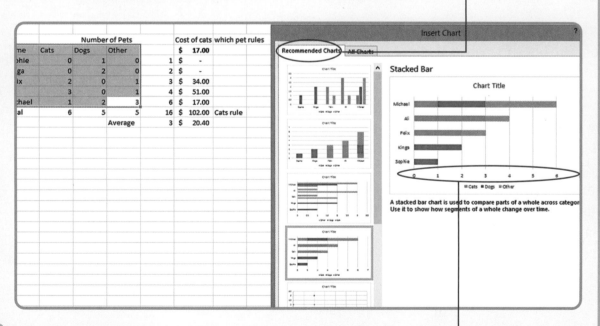

3 **Excel** recommends bar charts, maybe because you can easily see how many different types of pets each friend has.

Speed through charts

Easy access Chart Tools

The Chart Elements, Chart Styling and Chart filters buttons, with easy access to lots of options, save you going up to the Ribbon to work.

1 Open the *Basketball* spreadsheet and use **Recommended Charts** to create a 'Stacked Area' chart.

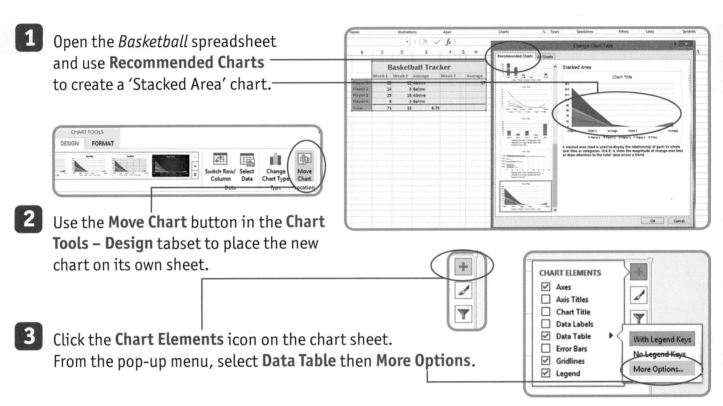

2 Use the **Move Chart** button in the **Chart Tools – Design** tabset to place the new chart on its own sheet.

3 Click the **Chart Elements** icon on the chart sheet. From the pop-up menu, select **Data Table** then **More Options**.

4 The **Format Data Table** pane appears and displays all choices. Try coloring text in the table, or **Horizontal table gridlines** only.

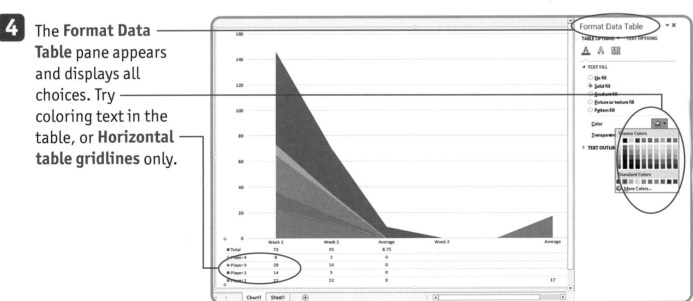

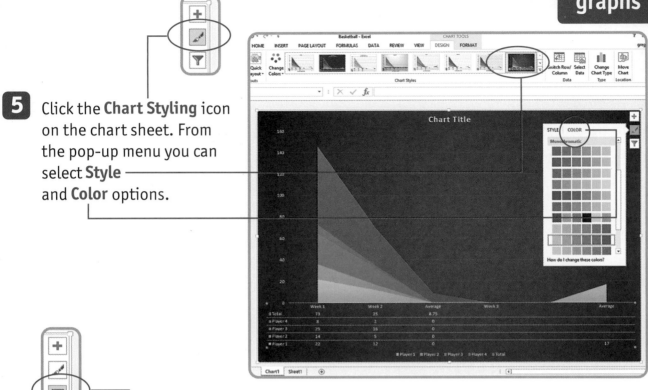

5 Click the **Chart Styling** icon on the chart sheet. From the pop-up menu you can select **Style** and **Color** options.

6 The **Chart Filters** icon lets you select and show smaller parts of the table information. From the pop-up menu, select **Values**.

7 Click to deselect **Total** and make sure **Week 1** and **Week 2** are the only categories ticked. Click **Apply**. Now the chart shows players' scores shrinking from *Week 1* to *Week 2*.

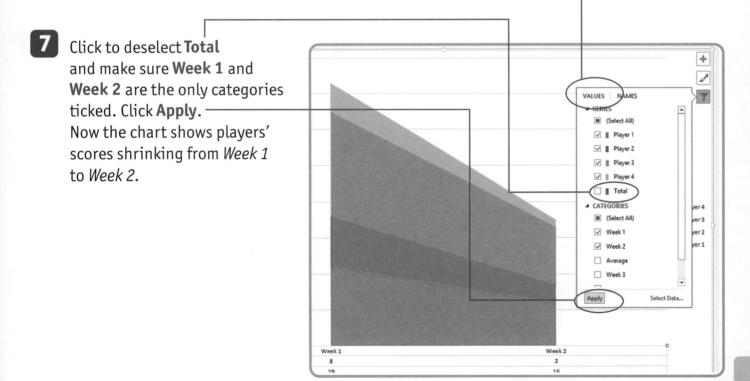

Using fast mini-graphs

Use **Sparklines** to see a quick set of charts and to be able to compare lots of number sets

This could be helpful for monthly figures of a class project, to see how well each person is doing

1 Select a **Row** of data for one person.

	A	B	C	D	E	F	G
1	Column1 ▾	May ▾	June ▾	July ▾	August ▾	Sep ▾	
2	Kathy	10	5	3	5	6	
3	Carol	5	7	5	8	3	
4	Zoey	6	8	10	12	8	
5	William	3	2	1	0	3	
6	Michael	8	9	9	7	4	

2 Click the **Insert** tab. In the 'Sparklines' toolset there are three choices. Click on the **Line** button.

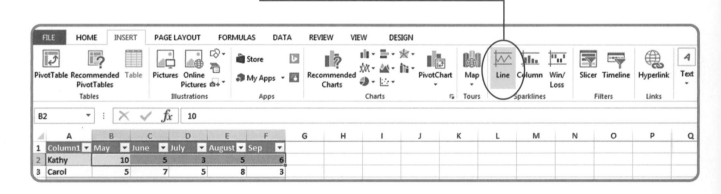

3 A dialog box appears. Click on the **Cell** you want the chart to appear in.

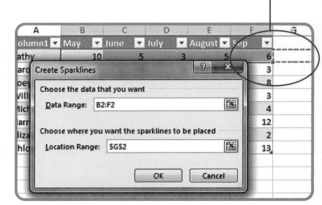

Create Sparklines

Choose the data that you want

Data Range: B2:F2

Choose where you want the sparklines to be placed

Location Range: G2

OK   Cancel

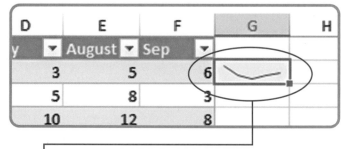

4 A **Sparkline** appears in the cell you have chosen.

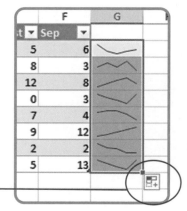

5 To see the Sparklines for everybody's figures on the table, click-and-drag on the **Fill handle**.

6 To make the Sparklines taller, click on the **Select All Cells** button. Then click-and-drag on a **vertical grid line** to make all cells taller.

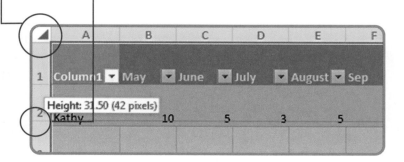

Top Tip!

To set a column of Sparklines to be in proportion, use the **Axis** button and select 'Same for all Sparklines'.

7 There are many options for how the Sparklines can look. Click on any Sparkline cell. Then click on the **Design** tab. Then click on **High Point** and **Low Point**. Red dots will appear on the Sparklines.

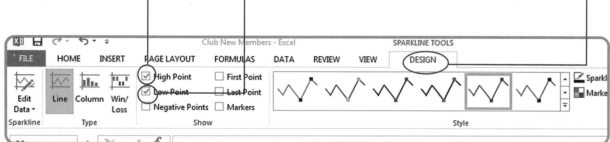

Show it quickly

Understand the numbers quickly with the **Quick Analysis tool**

The Quick Analysis tool gives you many choices for visualizing your data in a table and seeing any trends.

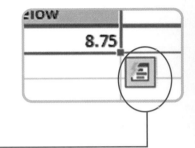

1 Open the *Basketball* spreadsheet and select part of the table. The **Quick Analysis** tool icon appears at the bottom right.

2 Click on the icon and select **Formatting – Data Bars.** Bars showing quantities appear in the cells.

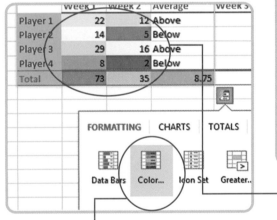

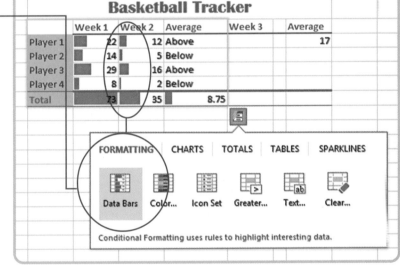

3 Or click on **Color.** Excel creates a range of colors in the cells. The stronger the color, the higher the value.

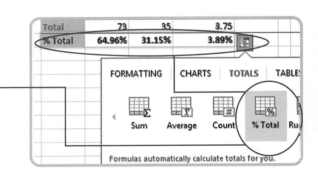

4 For a percentage analysis try **Totals – % Total.** Totals with percentages appear below the table totals.

Class data project

Analyze your class survey

Quick Analysis tools will make the data much easier to follow.

1 Create another table in *Class survey* spreadsheet. Add the class members' names to column **A**. In cells **A14** to **H14**, type the days of the week. Add the title.

	Monday	Tuesday	Wednesday	Thursday	Friday	Saturday	Sunday	
13			How many hours spent with your pets					
16 Sophie	2	1	0	2	1	0	0	
17 Kinga	1	2	3	1	3	2	4	
18 Felix	1	1	1	1	2	3	4	
19 Ali	4	4	4	4	4	4	4	
20 Michael	1	4	3	2	1	0	1	

2 Select the names and hours part of the table and use the **Quick Analysis** tool icon to select 'Sparklines'. Does the **Column** or **Line** option work better for this table?

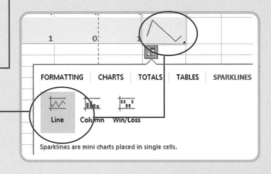

FORMATTING CHARTS TOTALS TABLES SPARKLINES

Line Column Win/Loss

Sparklines are mini charts placed in single cells.

3 Try the **Greater than** option. This colors cells that have higher than average numbers.

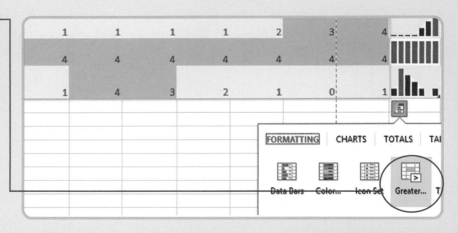

FORMATTING CHARTS TOTALS TA...

Data Bars Color... Icon Set Greater... T

Rich data labels

Add to your chart information with **Data Callouts**

Data Callouts are labels that you, or Excel, can add to your charts and style to make the information look more exciting.

1 Open the *Average Temperatures* spreadsheet and create a line chart using **Recommended Charts**. Move it to a chart sheet.

2 Right-click on the 'Max' line and select **Add Data Callouts**. Increase the font size in the labels.

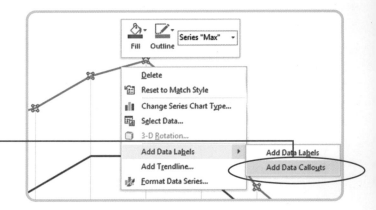

3 In **Chart Tools – Format** change the **Shape Styles**, and from the **Change Shape** drop-down menu select a Callout with a point.

4 Move the Callout labels away from the line. They now point to the place on the line that they refer to.

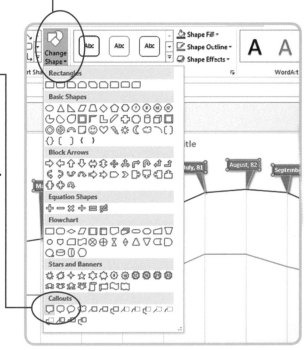

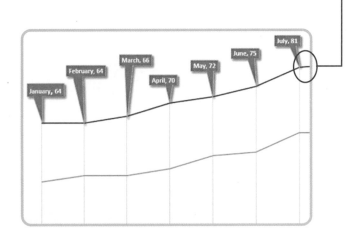

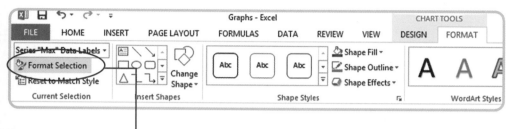

5 Click **Format Selection**; the 'Format Data Labels' pane appears.
Under 'Label Options' select **Value From Cells**
and **Select Range** if you want to show a different temperature.

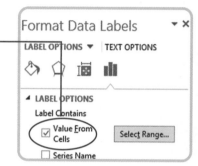

6 Add and style 'drop-down' bars from the **Chart Elements** icon and
the 'Format Down Bars' pane options.

7 Add a label for something unusual on the chart.
In **Chart Tools – Format** tab, on the **Insert Shapes** drop-down
menu, select a Callout with a point.

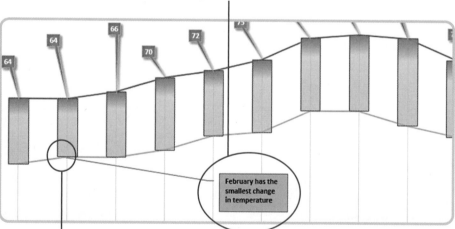

February has the
smallest change
in temperature

8 Edit the line to point to where you want it.
To add text, click on the box and select **Text Box** in **Drawing Tools**.

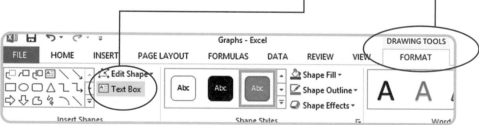

A slice of table

Chop up your data with the **Slicer** tool

**The Slicer is great for finding patterns in your table.
It works really well for big tables.**

1 Open the *Rehearsal Schedule* and fill in
times of attendance. Click **Format as Table**
on the **Home** tab.

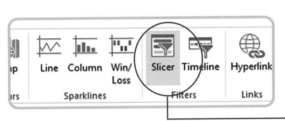

FIRST NAME (ROLE)	03/01/	03/02/	03/03/	03/04/	03/05/	03/06/	03/07/	03/08/	03/09/
65 Aaron (Oaken)	65	30	65	30	65	15	65	30	65
60 Carl (Hans)	60	60	0	60	60	30	30	0	60
80 Jane (Elsa)	80	10	0	80	80	20	80	0	80
55 Jose (Kristoff)	55	55	55	0	55	55	20	55	0
55 Joseph (Duke of Weselton)	55	15	55	55	55	20	15	0	55
90 Melissa (Anna)	90	70	90	0	90	10	90	50	90
95 Peter (Olaf)	95	65	95	95	95	0	30	0	95
50 Rebecca (Sven)	50	50	50	50	50	50	15	50	50
55 Zoya (Marshmallow)	55	55	55	55	55	55	55	55	55

ATTENDANCE TIME REHEARSING

2 Click on the table and on the **Insert** tab click on the **Slicer** button.
A dialog box appears. Select *03/08/16* and click **OK**.

3 Two of the players say they rehearsed for 55 minutes that day.
Check if this is true by clicking *55* on the **Slicer**.

Insert Slicers

- [ ] FIRST NAME (ROLE)
- [ ] 03/01/16
- [ ] 03/02/16
- [ ] 03/03/16
- [ ] 03/04/16
- [ ] 03/05/16
- [ ] 03/06/16
- [ ] 03/07/16
- [x] 03/08/16

4 The two players' rows showing attendance times appear.
It is true, they rehearsed for 55 minutes.

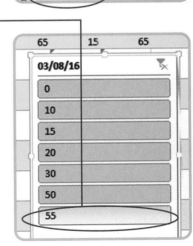

03/08/16

| 0 |
| 10 |
| 15 |
| 20 |
| 30 |
| 50 |
| 55 |

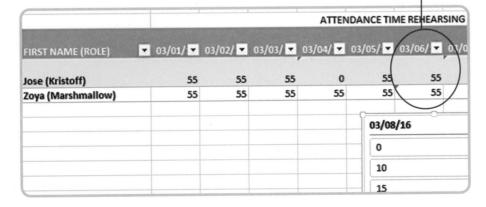

ATTENDANCE TIME REHEARSING

FIRST NAME (ROLE)	03/01/	03/02/	03/03/	03/04/	03/05/	03/06/	03/0
Jose (Kristoff)	55	55	55	0	55	55	
Zoya (Marshmallow)	55	55	55	55	55	55	

03/08/16

| 0 |
| 10 |
| 15 |

Class data project

Richly label then slice the survey

Add Data Callouts for anything unusual and then Slice to double check.

1 Create a chart from the new table in the Class survey spreadsheet. Add axes titles.

2 In the **Chart Tools – Format tab** choose **Insert Shapes**. From the drop-down menu select a Callout with a point and style.

3 Add text with the **Text Box** button in the **Insert Shapes** toolset.

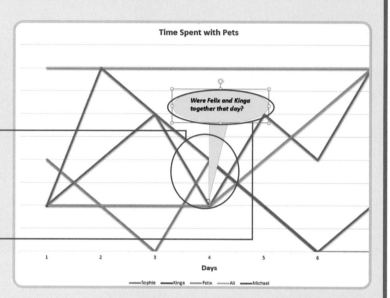

4 Go back to the chart. Click in the table and click on **Slicer**. In the dialog box, select 'Thursday' (column 5). Click **1** on the 'Slicer' pane. Two friends spent one hour with their pets on Thursday.

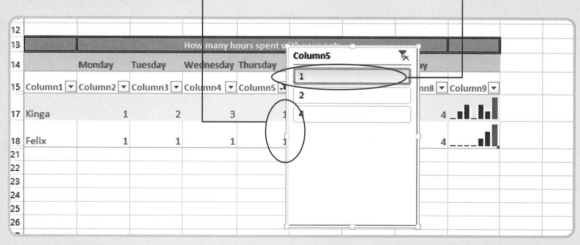

Pivot your chart

See your data from any angle with PivotTables
and PivotCharts

PivotTables and Charts are great for comparing different data sets.

1 Select part of the table. On the **Insert** tab,
click **Recommended PivotTables**.

2 Choose a 'PivotTable' from the dialog box.

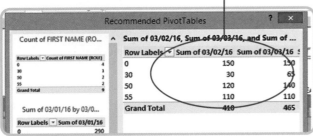

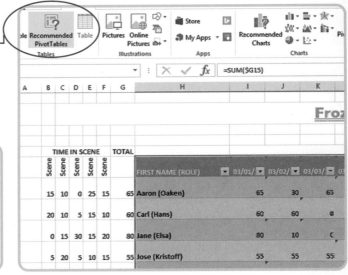

3 The **PivotTable Tools** tabset appears with an options 'field' to let you choose your data.
Here we have selected the first three days, showing times in rehearsal for each player.

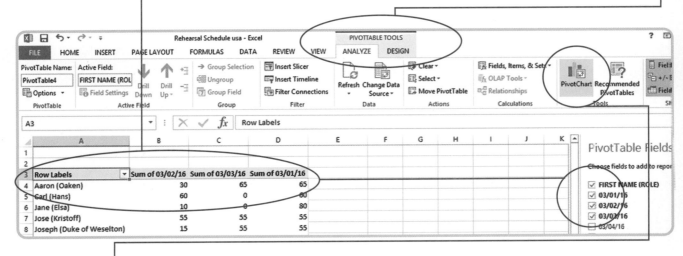

4 Click the **PivotChart** button.

5 Choose the best table from the 'Insert Chart' dialog box and then style with the **PivotChart Tools** tabset.

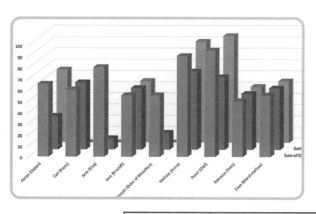 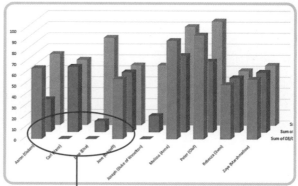

6 Change the viewing order of the days in the **PivotChart Fields** pane by clicking and dragging the **Values** fields and changing the order.

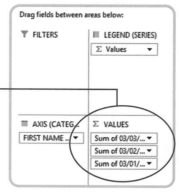

7 To compare only two players' rehearsal time over some days, click on the 'field' menu icon and select the players you want to compare. **Change Chart Type** to make it clearer.

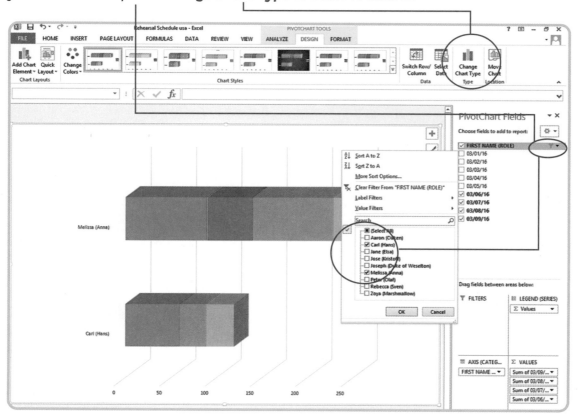

Adding graphics

Pictures and graphics can add interest to a spreadsheet

1 Click the **Pictures** button on the **Insert** tab. The 'Insert Picture' dialog box appears.

2 Find a picture on your computer, select it and click the **Insert** button.

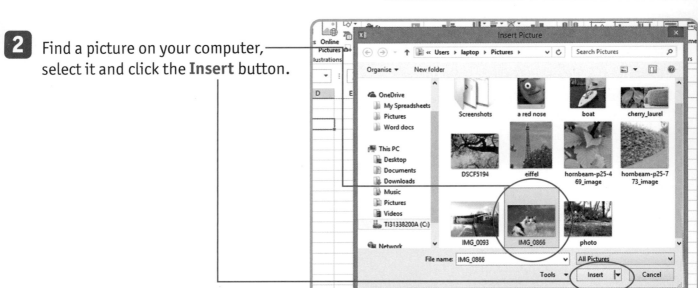

3 The picture appears on your worksheet. The **Picture Tools – Format** tab also opens on the Ribbon.

You can style it and add effects. This picture has a style that rounds off the corners and adds a reflection.

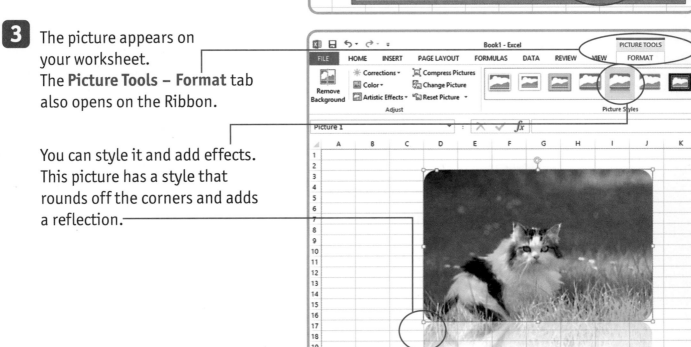

4 Specify the picture's size in the 'Size' toolset or click-and-drag the corners to resize it.

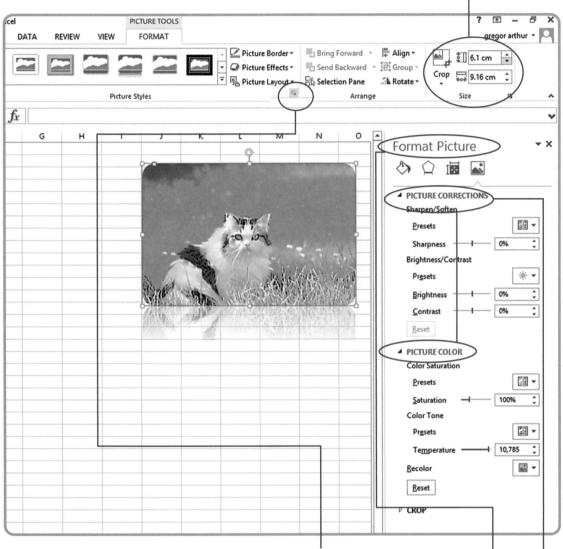

5 For more picture options click on the 'Picture Styles' toolset button. The 'Format Picture' pane appears.

You can make many changes to the picture including **Picture Corrections** and **Picture Color** options.

6 Click-and-drag the picture to move it around the worksheet.

Picture your PC

Use the clip tool to add a quick pic

Excel comes with a tool that allows you to take a quick snapshot of something on your computer.

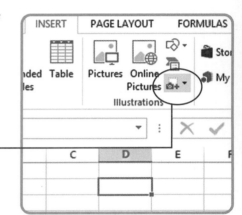

1 From the **Insert** tab, select the **Illustrations** toolset and click on the **Screenshot** tool.

2 The drop-down menu shows all the windows you have open.

3 Select the window you want and an image of it will be inserted in your worksheet.

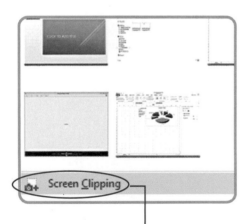

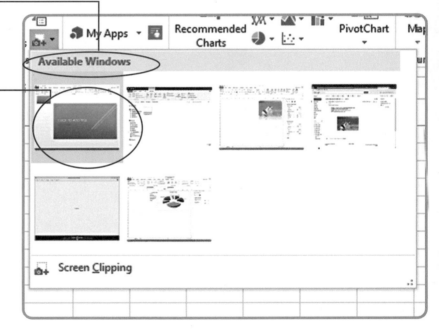

4 Select the **Screen Clipping** tool from the drop-down menu if you only want to capture part of the screen.

5 The window you want appears and the screen goes opaque. Click-and-drag the mouse over the area you want to capture and that image will be inserted into your worksheet.

Class presentation project

Clip with Excel to create an icon

Your presentation needs a cover page. With digital cameras, it couldn't be easier. Use the clip tool to illustrate your cover.

1 Add a new worksheet at the beginning of the presentation workbook.

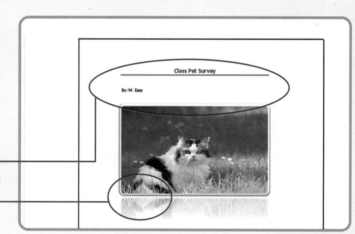

2 Add a title, your name and a picture. Move it below your title and resize it to fit.

3 Format the picture with a border. Preview your page and adjust the layout to fit it on to one page.

4 Open your school's website. Switch back to *Class presentation* and click on the **Screenshot** button.

5 Click on the **Screen Clipping** button. Clip the school logo from the website.

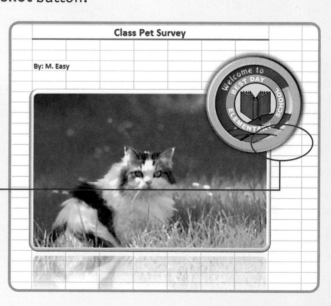

6 Position and size it on your presentation. Give it a border style to help it fit.

Text effects

Using WordArt to create high-impact lettering

Use 'WordArt' for very noticeable text. 'WordArt' can only be applied to text boxes, not text in a cell.

1 Click the **Text** button drop-down menu on the **Insert** tab. Select a 'WordArt' style.

2 A text box appears containing the words *Your Text Here*. Type over them with your own heading *My Excel Spreadsheet*.

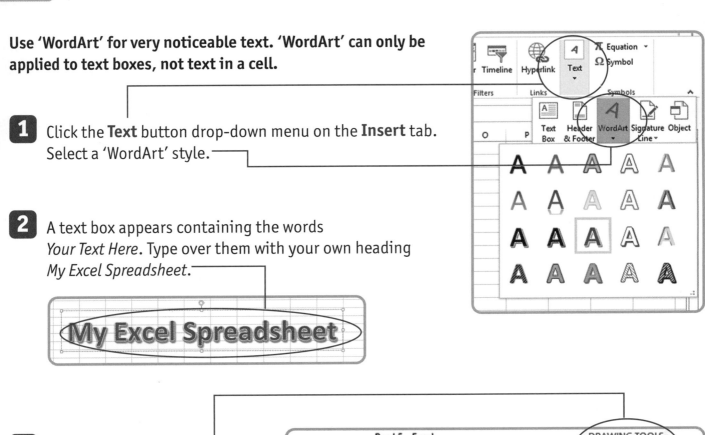

3 The **Drawing Tools – Format** tab also appears.

4 As with charts, the **Format** tab allows you to add some really clever effects. The text box now has a **Fill Theme** and a 'Preset' **Shape Effect** has been added.

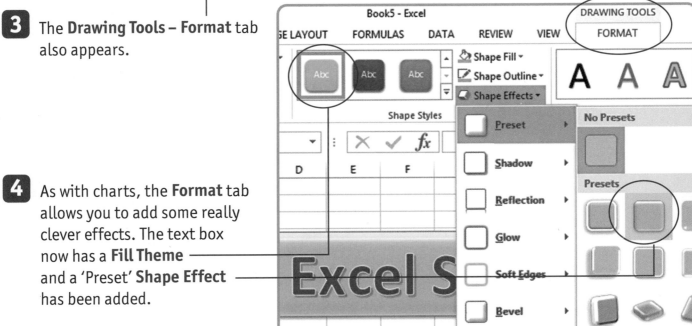

5 To see more exciting options, click on any toolset button in the **Format** tabset.

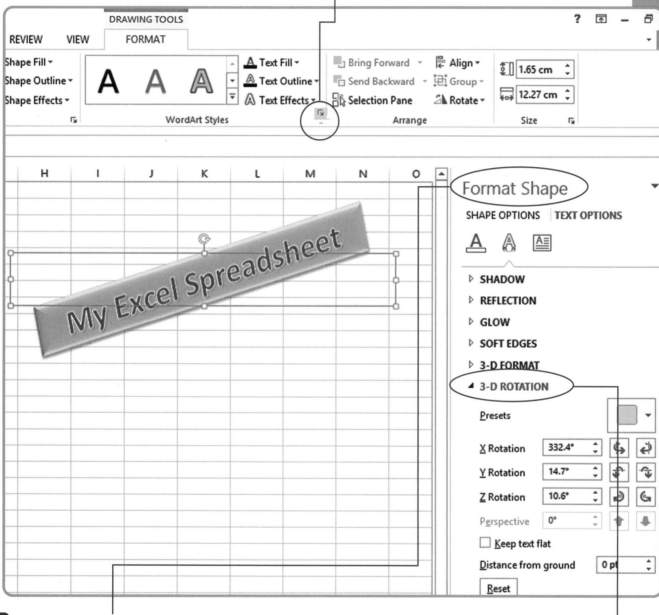

6 The 'Format Shape' pane appears. Explore the choices given
to create interesting effects. Try **3-D Rotation**.

Top Tip!

You can also add 'Clip Art',
'Shapes' and 'SmartArt' in the
Illustrations toolset.

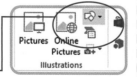

Print headers

Using Headers and Footers

'Headers' and 'Footers' exist at the top and bottom of every printed page. You can add a story title or page numbers.

1 Click the **Header & Footer** button on the **Insert** tab.

2 The **Header & Footer Tools – Design** tab opens on the Ribbon and the worksheet goes to 'Page Layout' mode.

3 Click into the footer or click the **Go to Header** button.

4 Headers and footers are split into left, right and center areas. Click on one and use the **Sheet Name** button. The code *&[TAB]* appears.

5 Replace the code with your header or footer name. You can style it up. Click outside the header when it's done.

6 Click on the 'Normal' selector in the status bar to return to the usual view of the worksheet. Check how it will look when printed with 'Print Preview'.

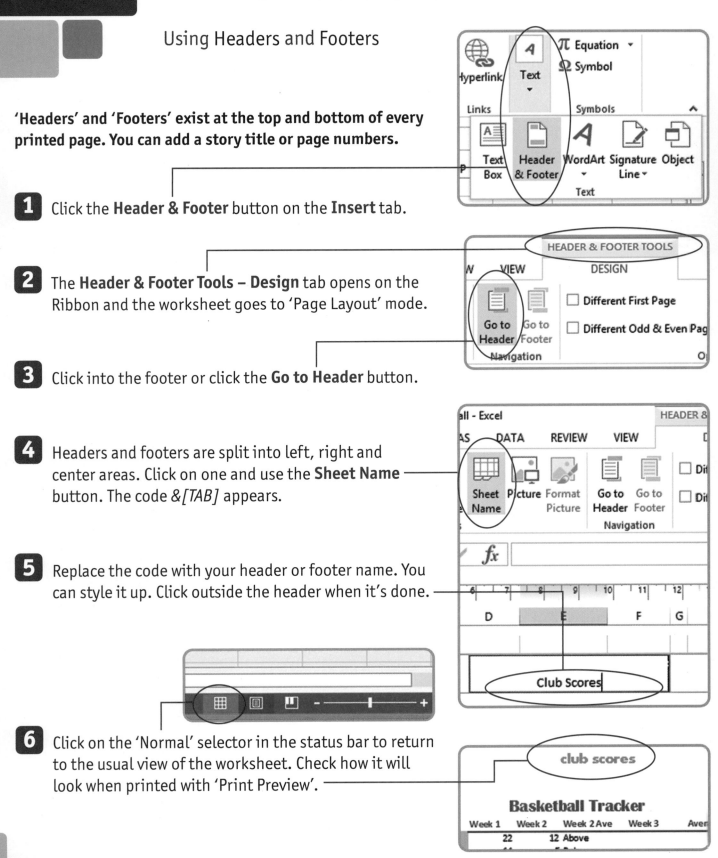

Class presentation project

Add a stunning heading, and numbers

Use WordArt to style your heading. The survey page will also need headers and footers.

1 On your cover sheet, delete the title and replace it with 'WordArt'.

2 Click the **Shape Effects** button drop-down menu and select **3-D Rotation**. Select a 'Parallel' option.

3 Click the **Header & Footer** button. Click in the left-hand section of the header and then click the **Sheet Name** button. This adds the worksheet name to every page.

4 Insert the date in the right-hand section of the header using the **Current Date** button.

5 Click **Go to Footer** and add then use the **page number** button. Print your table.

Quick chart change

Use Quick Layout for instant layout change

Quick Layout can save you lots of time if you want to see different layouts for your chart.

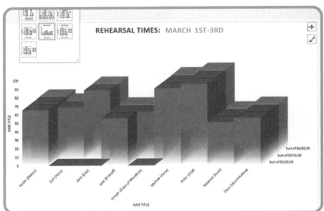

1 On a chart, use the **Quick Layout** button from the **PivotChart Tools – Design** tabset.

2 **Excel** suggests several different layouts. As you move through the selections the chart is rearranged with some interesting choices.

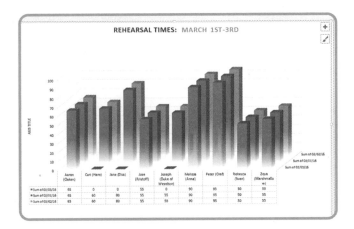

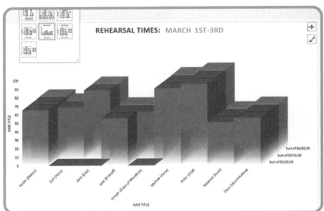

3 Try **Quick Layout** on some of your other charts.

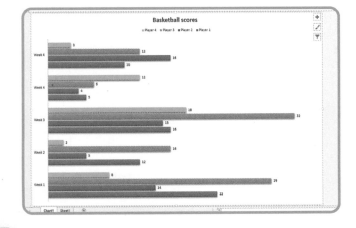

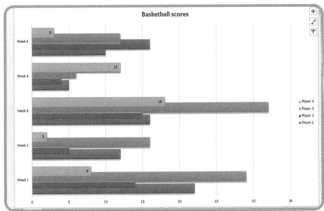

Future bookings

Use Date functions to work out time between dates

Your play was a success. You have been asked to do another show and have been given several dates.

1 On a new spreadsheet, enter today's date and three *Show Dates*.
To work out the number of days until each show date, simply subtract
the *Now* cell **A2** from the *Show date* cell **B2**.

	A	B	C	D
1	Now	Show Dates	DAYS	
2	March 4, 2016	September 8, 2016	=SUM(B2-A2)	
3	March 4, 2016	November 12, 2016	SUM(number1, [number2],	
4	March 4, 2016	January 7, 2017		
5				

	A	B	C	D
1	Now	Show Dates	DAYS	
2	March 4, 2016	September 8, 2016	188	
3	March 4, 2016	November 12, 2016	253	
4	March 4, 2016	January 7, 2017	309	
5				

2 But now you need to know how many weekdays, not
weekend days, you have left. On the **Formulas** tab,
click the **Date & Time** drop-down menu and select
Networkdays.

PAGE LAYOUT FORMULAS DATA

Financial Logical Text Date & Lookup & Ma
Time ▾ Reference ▾ Tr

Function Library

DATE
DATEVALUE
DAY
DAYS
DAYS360
EDATE
EOMONTH
HOUR
ISOWEEKNUM
MINUTE
MONTH
NETWORKDAYS
NETWORKDAYS.I

3 A box appears. Click on the *Now* and *Show Date* cells to enter
into the 'Start_date' and 'End_date' fields.

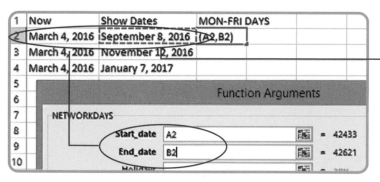

4 The number of days without weekends appears.
Autofill the other show dates.

1	Now	Show Dates	MON-FRI DAYS
2	March 4, 2016	September 8, 2016	135
3	March 4, 2016	November 12, 2016	181
4	March 4, 2016	January 7, 2017	221
5			

Sharing online

Invite people to Share documents

**If you need more people to help on your project, sharing means
it all happens on one document in one place.**

1 Open a document and click on the **File** tab.
Select **Save As** and **Add a Place**
and then **Office 365 SharePoint** or
OneDrive.

2 You will be asked to sign in to your
account. Once that's done,
create a folder location.

3 In the 'Save As' pane, your new location will appear.
Save your file to that location.

4 The first time you want to share a document online,
select **Share** and **Invite People** and then **Save to Cloud**.

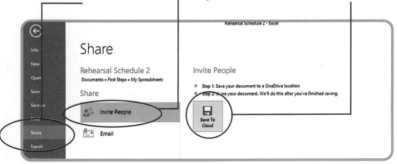

5 The **Invite People** pane appears. This is where you send out invites to share.

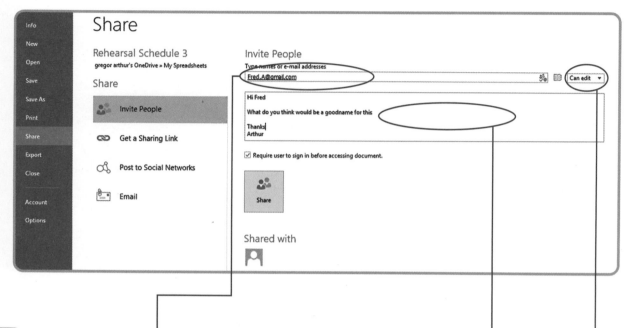

6 Type in **email addresses** of the people you are inviting to share.

7 Type an invite message into the **message field**.

8 Select from the drop-down menu **Can edit** or **Can view** only.

9 Check if you want invitees to **sign in** with the password you give. Then click **Share**.

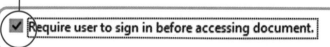

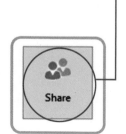

No Excel?

Export, Open and view PDFs

Your work can be opened by someone who hasn't got Excel. A PDF is a file that can be opened easily.

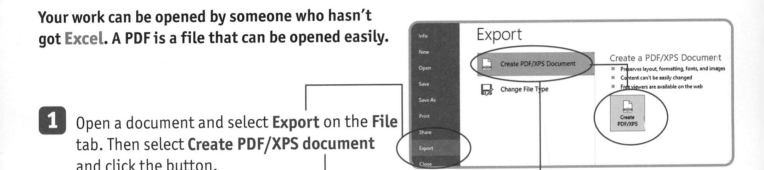

1 Open a document and select **Export** on the **File** tab. Then select **Create PDF/XPS document** and click the button.

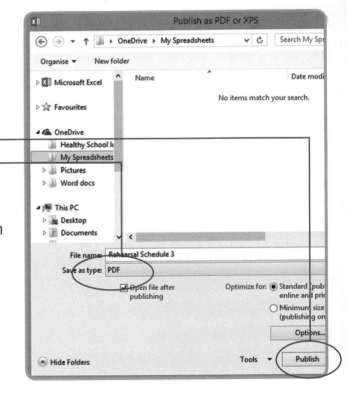

2 A dialog box appears. Make sure 'Save as type' is set to *PDF*, and click the **Publish** button.

3 You can open a **PDF**, but not in Excel. Find it with your computer file finder. It opens in *Adobe*.

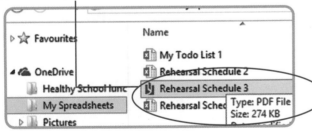

4 It may not look the same as the styling may have changed but it is useful to people without **Excel**.

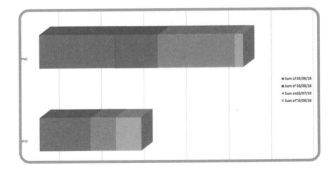

Class presentation project

Get your work out online

You and your friends are checking your class survey. Share your class survey online with them.

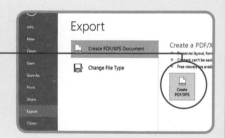

1 Open *Class survey* and click on the **File** tab. Select **Save As** and then your Cloud **OneDrive** location. Click **Browse** to create a new online folder *My class survey*. Save the document.

2 Select **Export** on the **File** tab. Select **Create PDF/XPS document** and press the **Publish** button. Save the **PDF** into the *My class survey* folder.

3 The first time you want to share the PDF online, select **Share** and **Invite People** and then click the **Save to Cloud** button.

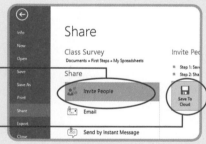

4 Type in **email addresses** of the people you are inviting to share. Type an invite message into the **message field.**

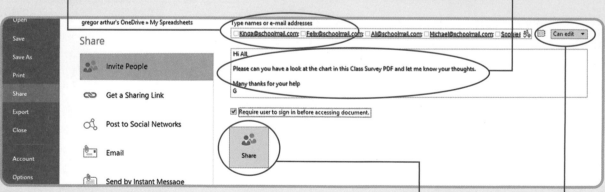

5 Select from the drop-down menu **Can view**. Click the **Share** button.

Can anybody help me?

You may be asked to **comment** on a document created by someone else

Open the shared document on OneDrive.

1 Click on the **Review** tab and then the **Track Changes** button. Select **Highlight Changes**.

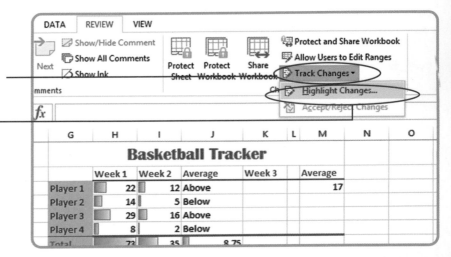

2 The 'Highlight Changes' dialog box appears. Click on *Track changes while editing*.

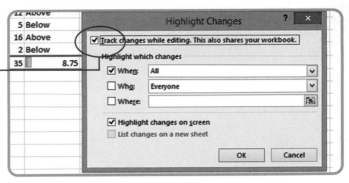

3 Make your changes. Each changed cell is bordered blue with a blue triangle.

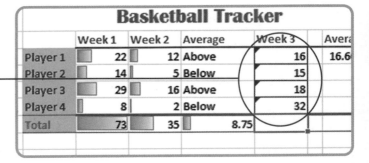

4 To keep or remove changes select the **Track Changes** button. Then **Accept/Reject changes**.

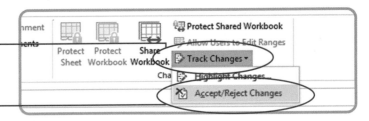

5 A dialog box appears. Click **OK**.
The next box, 'Accept or Reject changes', appears. Work through the changes clicking on **Accept** or **Reject**.

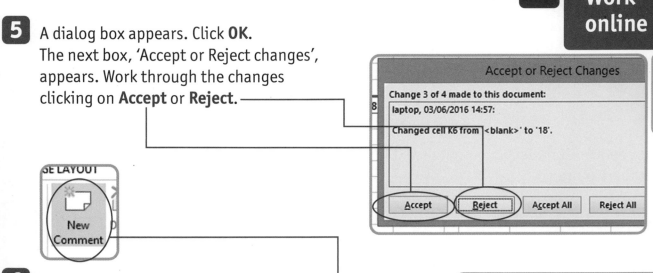

6 Select a rejected cell and press the **New Comment** button. The cell now has a red triangle. Type into the comment box.

7 Use the **Show/Hide** and **Show All Comments** buttons to work through. Use **Edit Comment** to change a comment.

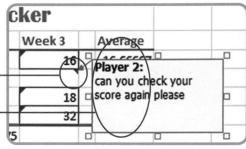

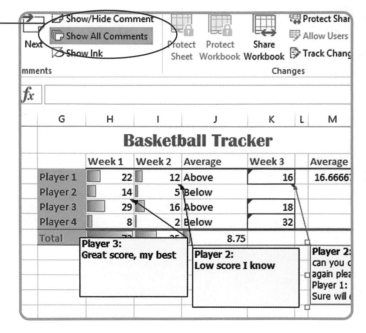

8 Click on a red triangle cell and click **Delete** to remove the comments.

9 Select **Highlight Changes** to switch off track changes.

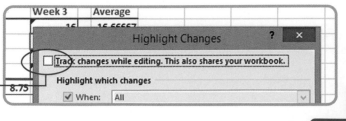

Help is always there

Did we lose you on one of the projects?

Top Tip!

Press the **F1** key to pop-up 'Help' buttons.

Excel has help built in. If you are connected to the Internet there is more.

1 To get 'Help', click the **?** icon.

2 Type your question into the search field and click **Search**.

3 If you are on the Internet, 'Help' will show answers to your question, including videos.

4 If the connection is slow or not working, you can change the connection status manually by clicking on the button at the top of the pop-up.

5 If you are not connected, you will see only help that is built into the program.

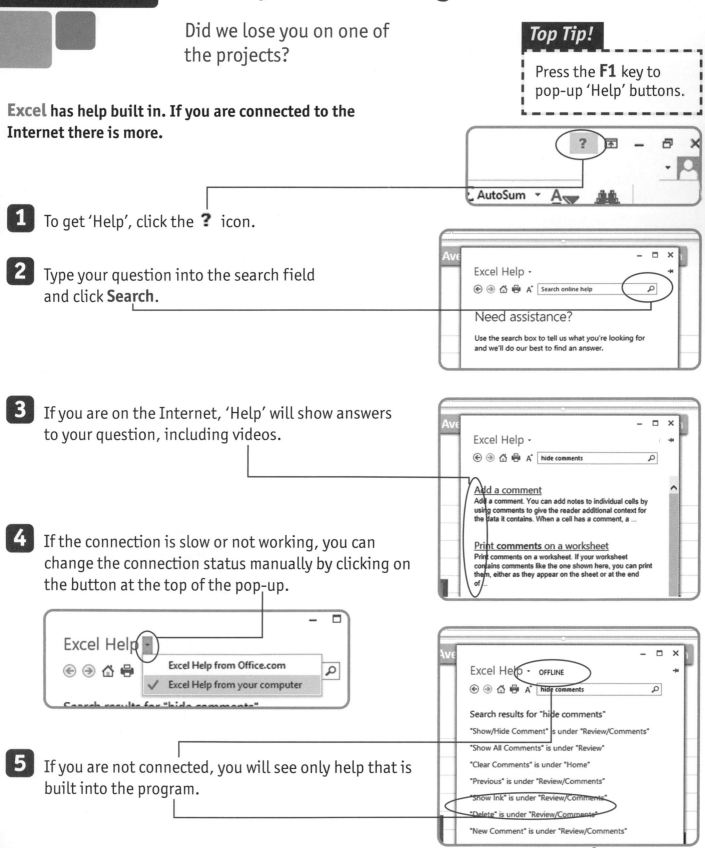

Using the help menus project

Get yourself some help!

There are lots more tools to look at. Use Help to find out about them.

1 Search for help on the **SmartArt** button.

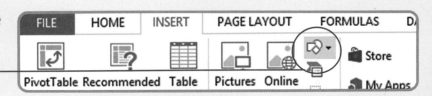

FILE | HOME | INSERT | PAGE LAYOUT | FORMULAS | D/

PivotTable | Recommended | Table | Pictures | Online | Store | My Apps

2 How can you add a 'Hyperlink'?

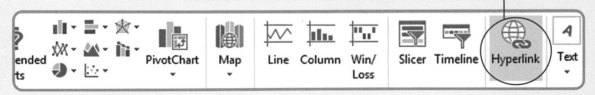

ended ts | PivotChart | Map | Line | Column | Win/Loss | Slicer | Timeline | Hyperlink | Text

3 How do you 'hide comments'?

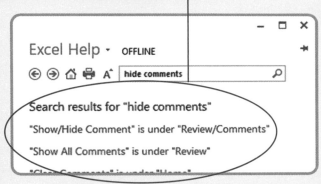

Excel Help · OFFLINE

hide comments

Search results for "hide comments"

"Show/Hide Comment" is under "Review/Comments"

"Show All Comments" is under "Review"

4 How can you stop other people changing your document?

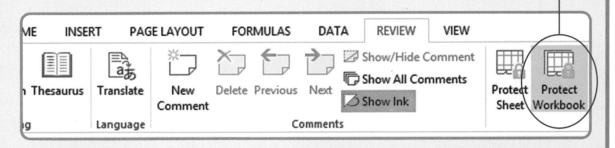

ME | INSERT | PAGE LAYOUT | FORMULAS | DATA | REVIEW | VIEW

Thesaurus | Translate | New Comment | Delete | Previous | Next | Show/Hide Comment | Show All Comments | Show Ink | Protect Sheet | Protect Workbook

g | Language | Comments

Index

Add Chart Element 72, 74
Add Data Callouts 88
Add to Print Area 39
Align Text 23
All Borders 32
All Charts 80
Autofill 103
Autofit Column Width 24
AutoSum 62–3
Average 37, 62
Axis Titles 72

Back Wall 77
Blank workbook 10
Bold 22, 25
Borders 32, 35
Browse 12

Can edit 105
Can view 105, 107
Category 4, 14
Cell 84
Cell Format 25
Cell Reference 58
Cell Style 34–5
Change Chart Type 93
Change Shape 88
Chart Elements 75–6, 79, 82, 89
Chart filters 82–3
Chart Styling 82–3
Chart Tools 70–2, 76
Charts 92
Clear Print Area 39
Click-and-drag 6
Clipboard 48–9
Close 4, 13, 49
Color 86
Color 83
Column 26, 27, 70, 87
Comma Style 66
Copy 44, 47
Create 14
Create PDF/XPS document 106–7
Current Date 101
Custom 69
Custom Sort 28–9

Data 30
Data Callouts 88, 91
Data Labels 74, 77
Data Table 74, 77, 82
Date 69
Date & Time 103
Decrease Decimal 65, 67

Delete Cells 27
Design 37, 71–2, 78
Draw table tool 32
Drawing Tools 89

Edit Comment 109
Export 106, 107

File 10, 11, 38, 40, 104, 106–7
Fill Color 30, 33, 75
Fill handle 85
Fill Theme 98
Flash Fill 30–1
Floor 77
Font 20, 22
Format 24, 75–6, 78, 98–9
Format as Table 36, 90
Format Button 69
Format Cells 69
Format Data 82
Format Painter 52
Format Selection 75, 89
Formula Bar 4, 21
Formulas 64, 103

Go to Footer 101
Go to Header 100
Greater than button 87
Grow Font 20, 77

Header & Footer 100–1
Help 111
High Point 85
highlight 5, 108, 109
Home 20
Horizontal table gridlines 82
Hover-over 6
How to use this template 17
Hyperlink 53

Illustrations 96, 99
Increase Decimal 65
Insert 26, 29, 53, 70, 78, 90
Insert Cells 26, 29
Insert Chart 80–1
Insert Shapes 89, 91
Invite People 104–5, 107
Italic 22

Landscape 40–1
Layout 78
Legend 72
Line 84, 87
Line Color 32

Line Style 32
Link 14
Logical 67
Logical Function 64
Long Date 68
Low Point 85

Merge & Center 23, 25, 35

Networkdays 103
New Cell Style 34, 35
New Comment 109
New Sheet 19, 71
Number Format 65, 68

Office 365 SharePoint 104
OneDrive 12, 104, 108
Open 11
Order 28
Orientation 23

Page Layout 39
Page number 101
Paste Values 50–1
PDF 106
Percent Style 66
Picture Color 95
Picture Corrections 95
Pictures 94
Pie Chart 78, 81
PivotChart 92–3
PivotChart Fields 93
PivotChart Tools 93
PivotTables 92
Plot Area 75
Portrait Orientation 40
Print 38, 40, 42–3
Print Area 39
Print Preview 38, 40–2
Publish 106–7

Quick Access 46
Quick Access Toolbar 4
Quick Analysis 86–7
Quick Layout 102
Quick Print 43

Recommend Charts 82
Recommended Charts 80–1, 88
Recommended PivotTables 92
Redo 46
Reject 109
Review 54, 108
Ribbon 4

Row 26, 27, 84
Save 10
Save As 10–1, 104
Save to Cloud 104–5, 107
Screen Clipping 96–7
Screenshot 96–7
Search 110
Select Range 89
Series Options 79
Set Print Area 39
Shape Effect 98, 101
Share 88, 104, 105
Sheet Name 100, 107
Shift cells down 27, 29, 101
Short Date 26
Show All Comments 68
Show Margins 109
Show/Hide 38
Side Wall 20, 75
Slice 105
Slicer 90–1
SmartArt 91
Sort & Filter 28, 111
Sort A to Z 28
Sort by 28
Sparkline 28
Spelling 54, 85
Style 55
Sum 83

Tab 37
Table Tools 5
Tapping 37
Text 9, 31
Text Box 89, 98
Text Effects 91
Thesaurus 54, 77
Time 55
Toolset 69
Total 5
Touch/Mouse Mode 37
Track Changes 108

Underline 108
Undo 22

Value from cells 43
Values 83, 89
vertical grid line 93

Wrap Text 23, 25, 85

Zoom 4
Zoom to Page 38

ARCTURUS

This edition published in 2015 by Arcturus Publishing Limited
26/27 Bickels Yard, 151–153 Bermondsey Street,
London SE1 3HA

Copyright © Arcturus Holdings Limited

All rights reserved. No part of this publication may be reproduced, stored in a retrieval system, or transmitted, in any form or by any means, electronic, mechanical, photocopying, recording or otherwise, without prior written permission in accordance with the provisions of the Copyright Act 1956 (as amended). Any person or persons who do any unauthorised act in relation to this publication may be liable to criminal prosecution and civil claims for damages.

ISBN: 978-1-78404-971-3
AD004705US

Printed in China

Microsoft product screen shots reprinted with permission from Microsoft Corporation.

Microsoft, Word, Excel, and Windows are trademarks of the Microsoft group of companies.

Excel Made Easy is an independent publication and is not affiliated with, nor has it been authorized, sponsored, or otherwise approved by Microsoft Corporation.

The materials in this book relate to Microsoft Office 2013.

Prepared for Arcturus by Starfish Design Editorial and Project Management Ltd.